Basic
German

Course Book

Berlitz Publishing
New York London Singapore

Contacting the Editors
Every effort has been made to provide accurate information in this
publication, but changes are inevitable. The publisher cannot be
responsible for any resulting loss, inconvenience or injury. We would
appreciate it if readers would call our attention to any errors or
outdated information. We also welcome your suggestions.
Please contact us at: comments@berlitzpublishing.com

Cover and pack redesign © March 2013
Printed in China

Publishing Director: Mina Patria
managing Editor: Kate Drynan
Editorial Assistant: Sophie Cooper
Audio Producer: Paul Ruben Studio
Text: Dr. Steve Williams (Word Bank)
Language Adviser: Sabine Amoos
Teaching Adviser: Rosi McNab
Editors: Saskia Gorospe Rombouts, Sylvia Goulding, Peter Kellersman, Elvira Ortiz, Joachim Siebert
Cover Design: Beverley Speight
Interior Design: Max Crandall
Production Manager: Raj Trivedi
Illustrations: Mona Daly, Parrot Graphics, Andy Levine, Chris Reed
Maps: MAGELLAN Geographix

Acknowledgments

Thanks are due to the following individuals and organizations for their assistance during the location recordings in Berlin:
Professor Werner Dewitz of the Freie Universität Berlin for his assistance in organizing the location recordings;
Suzanne Ramshaw for her assistance to the Audio Producer; Anke Sontowski and Rabea Werner for conducting the interviews.
The following organizations kindly allowed us to record interviews with members of their staff on their premises: Café Kranzler (Wolf
Nowak); Avis Car Rental (Benno Kischel); T&M Verlag (Dr. Harald Böttcher); Übersee Reisebüro (Uwe Klapka); UTTA Reisebüro (H.
Youssef); Kempinski Hotel Bristol; Potsdam Information (Gabi Weidner); KaDeWe (Karin Tauer); Peek & Cloppenburg (Herr Großjoh
Flughafen Tegel.

Contents

Unit **1** is about meeting people and giving information about yourself. By the end, you will know how to:

- greet people and say goodbye
- introduce yourself
- spell your name and give your telephone number
- ask somebody's name
- say where you're from

Guten Tag!

1

Word Bank

Abend	*evening*	ich heiße	*I'm (called)/my name is*
ach	*oh*	Ihnen	*(to) you*
auch	*also*	ist	*is*
Auf Wiederhören.	*Goodbye (on the phone).*	mein	*my*
Auf Wiedersehen.	*Goodbye.*	mich	*me*
danke	*thank you*	Morgen	*morning*
es	*it*	Nacht	*night*
Familienname	*surname; last name*	Name	*name*
Frau	*Mrs./Ms.*	sehr gut	*very well*
Freut mich!	*Pleased to meet you! (literally: pleases me)*	Sie	*you (formal)*
gut	*good; well*	Tag	*day*
Gute Nacht!	*Good night!*	Tschüs!	*Bye (informal)!*
Guten Abend!	*Good evening!*	und	*and*
Guten Morgen!	*Good morning!*	Und Ihnen?	*And you?*
Guten Tag	*Hello, good morning/ afternoon!*	Versuchen Sie es!	*You try it!*
Hallo!	*Hi!*	Vorname	*first name*
Herr	*Mr.*	wie	*how*
ich	*I*	Wie geht es Ihnen?	*How are you?*
		Wie geht's?	*How are you? (informal)*

Freut mich!

Greeting people and giving your name

RECORDING *Listen carefully to the introductions and repeat.*

Guten Tag!

Guten Morgen!

Guten Abend!

Auf Wiedersehen!

Tschüs!

Gute Nacht!

RECORDING
1. *Listen to the recording, and then decide whether the speakers are saying hello or goodbye, and what time of day it is (if it is mentioned).*

RECORDING *Before doing Activity 2, listen to the recording to find out how to introduce yourself in German.*

RECORDING
2. *Find the two pictures that fit each conversation. Watch out: there's one picture too many!*

a. „Guten Tag. Ich heiße Fritz Knoll."

b. „Freut mich. Thomas Storch."

c. „Bernd Krüger. Freut mich."

d. „Ich heiße Horst Henneberg."

e. „Guten Abend. Gisela Kalisch."

f. „Irene Pfaff. Freut mich."

g. „Guten Tag. Ich heiße Birgit Walther."

3. *You are checking into a hotel. Fill the gaps with appropriate responses.*

Receptionist: Guten Tag. Wie kann ich Ihnen helfen?

You: _____ _____. *(Greeting)*

Ich _____ _____. *(Give your name.)*

Receptionist: Wie bitte? Wie ist Ihr Familienname?

You: Mein _____ ist _____.

Receptionist: Und Ihr Vorname?

You: Mein _____ ist _____.

Receptionist: Danke.

Wie bitte?
I'm sorry?/Pardon? (Literally: How please?)

Wie ist Ihr Familienname/Vorname?
What's your last name/first name? (Literally: How is...)

Wie kann ich Ihnen helfen?
How can I help you?

Now listen to the rest of the recording for this section.

4. *Fill in the gaps in this conversation between Herr Schmidt and his colleague, Herr Hartmann:*

Schmidt: Guten Tag, Herr Hartmann!

Wie _____ _____ _____?

Hartmann: Sehr _____, _____. Und _____?

Schmidt: Ach, ich kann nicht klagen.

Ich kann nicht klagen.   *I can't complain.*

Close up

The letter ß

The letter **ß** indicates a sharper "s" sound. Its pronunciation is similar to the ss in English. Usually the ß is preceded by a long vowel (e.g., **Straße, Fuß,** etc.).
ss is used when it is preceeded by a short vowel (**Wasser, Kasse**), in upper case words (**FUSS**), or when typewriters and keyboards are not equipped with the ß letter.

Verbs

When you look up verbs in a dictionary, you'll notice that most of them end in **-en**. (This verb form is called the _infinitive_.) For example: **heißen** is the verb "to be called."

However, "I am called" is **ich heiße**—without the **-n**! This is because the ending of a German verb changes according to whether the subject is "I," "we," "you," "he/she/it," or "they." We'll be explaining this in more detail later in the unit.

Wie ist Ihre Nummer?

Spelling your name and giving your telephone number

Listen to the alphabet in German before attempting Activity 1.

1. **Circle the names below that you hear spelled.**

Erika	Petra
Hannelore	Sabine
Karl	Sibylle
Käthe	Susanne
Kerstin	Sylvia
Klaus	Walter
Peter	Werner

Now look again at the names you have circled and try to spell them out loud.

Word Bank

buchstabieren	*to spell*	nein	*no*
erreichen	*to reach*	neu	*new*
hier	*here*	nicht	*not*
im Moment	*at the moment*	Nummer	*number*
ja	*yes*	spricht	*speaks, is speaking*
kann (er/sie/es kann)	*can*	wiederholen	*to repeat*
können (Sie können)	*can*	zuhören	*to listen*
Magazin	*magazine*	zurückrufen	*to call back*
natürlich	*of course, naturally*		

2. *Listen to the recording, then write down the last names you hear. When you've done that, spell your own first name and last name out loud in German.*

Listen to the numbers 0–10 before attempting Activity 3.

Numbers 0–10

0 null		**3** drei		**6** sechs		**9** neun
1 eins		**4** vier		**7** sieben		**10** zehn
2 zwei/zwo*		**5** fünf		**8** acht		

* **zwo** *is used when giving numbers on the phone, to avoid confusion with* **drei**.

3. *Which of these business cards belong to the people taking part in the telephone conversation?*

Ja.   Yes.
Nein.   No.

Tempo Magazin
Petra Lenz

Priesterweg 10,□
13151 Berlin□
Telefon 030 181 9000

a.

Tempo Magazin
Dieter Schulz

Priesterweg 10,□
13151 Berlin□
Telefon 030 181 9510

b.

ABC Werbung
Petra Lenz

Uhlandweg 101,□
13180 Berlin□
Telefon 030 319 1510

c.

Sind Sie . . . ?   *Are you . . . ?*

. . . ist im Moment nicht hier.   *. . . isn't here at the moment.*

Kann er mich zurückrufen?   *Can he phone me back?*

Practice **ja, nein** *and* **nicht** *on the recording before continuing with the next activity.*

4. **Sie sind dran!** *It's your turn! Imagine that you are phoning Tempo Magazin. You want to speak to Herr Schulz. Make sure that you can spell your name and give your phone number in German before you play the recording.*

Es tut mir leid.   *I'm sorry.*

5. *Listen to the answering machine messages, and then look at Gisela Braun's phone pad. Correct any numbers that are wrong.*

Hier spricht...
It's... speaking.

A bis Z Versicherung
A–Z Insurance (name of company)

Ich bin's.
It's me.

Ciao!
Bye! (Italian–very informal in German)

Ich bin unter... zu erreichen.
You can reach me at...

A-Z Versicherung
314 8818

Herzog, Marion
313 2900

Pfaff, Gudrun
815 7482

Schmidt, Rudi
782 4141

6. *Mark which words in these sentences should begin with a capital letter.*

a. guten tag. mein name ist henneberg—horst henneberg.

b. guten abend, herr schmidt! wie geht es ihnen?

c. guten morgen. ich bin fritz knoll.

d. kommen sie herein.

Close-up

Verb endings

To use a verb with a subject in a sentence, you have to change the form of that verb (conjugate). In many cases, you take the **-en** ending off the infinitive, leaving the <u>stem</u> of the verb, then add the appropriate ending for the subject. For example, the verb "to be called" in German is **heißen**. The stem of **heißen** is **heiß-**. If you want to say "I am called," you add the ending **-e** to the stem: **ich heiße**. Here is the full present tense of **heißen**:

Singular

ich	heiß<u>e</u>	I	am called
du	heiß<u>t</u>	you (inf.)	are called
Sie	heiß<u>en</u>	you (form.)	are called
er/sie/es	heiß<u>t</u>	he/she/it	is called

Plural

wir	heiß<u>en</u>	we	are called
ihr	heiß<u>t</u>	you (inf.)	are called
Sie	heiß<u>en</u>	you (form.)	are called
sie	heiß<u>en</u>	they	are called

These verb endings are the same for almost all verbs—so you only have to learn them once.

Capital letters

Capitals are used more frequently in German than in English. They are used:

- at the beginning of a sentence (as in English)

- for proper nouns, e.g., people's names (as in English)

- for all other nouns, e.g., **Name** "name," **Tag** "day"

- for **Sie**, "you," **Ihnen**, "to you," and **Ihr**, "your"

The word for "I"—**ich**—doesn't have a capital (unless it comes at the beginning of a sentence).

Kommen Sie aus Berlin?

Saying where you are from

Word Bank

auf	on	München	Munich
aus	from; out (of)	Österreich	Austria
ausgezeichnet	excellent; very well	plus	plus
Bayern	Bavaria (German state or Land)	Polen	Poland
		recht gut	very well
Bern	Berne	Schleswig-Holstein	Schleswig-Holstein (German state or Land)
das	this; that		
dürfen (ich darf)	may	und	and
Geschäftsreise	business trip	Urlaub	vacation
im	in the	von	from; of
Köln	Cologne	vorstellen	to introduce
kommen	to come	Wien	Vienna
Land	German state; country	woher	where from
minus	minus		

Listen to the introduction before continuing.

1. *Match the people to the places on the map. Who might come from Zürich?*

Ich komme aus...
I come from...

Servus!
Hello! (Southern German/Austrian greeting and farewell)

Woher kommen Sie?
Where do you come from?

Mein Name ist...
My name is...

Practice the pronunciation of the countries before
continuing with Activity 2.

RECORDING

2.

Sie sind dran! *It's your turn! Introduce yourself, and say*
where you're from. Here are some country names to
help you.

Ich komme aus...	I come from...
Australien	Australia
den Vereinigten Staaten/den USA	the United States/the USA
England	England
Großbritannien	Great Britain
Irland	Ireland
Kanada	Canada
Neuseeland	New Zealand
Nordirland	Northern Ireland
Schottland	Scotland
Südafrika	South Africa
Wales	Wales

Did You Know?

German speakers are generally a little more formal in the way they address each other than English speakers. It's quite usual, and not unfriendly, for colleagues and neighbors to address each other by their last name, as **Herr Schmidt** or **Frau Braun**, rather than use their first names. However, the younger generation is more relaxed about this.

Frau is the title for all adult women, whether they are married or not. You should use the title **Fräulein**, "Miss," only to refer to a female child or adolescent—if at all.

3. *Where are these people from? Write the answers in English.*

Susan Bell:

Dieter Pohl:

Herr Nowakowski:

Otto Hinze:

Darf ich vorstellen?	May I introduce . . . ?
Das ist . . .	This/That is . . .
Sind Sie von hier?	Are you from here?

4. *You're on a plane to Germany. You're sitting next to a German speaker and would like to talk to her.*

(Say hello, and introduce yourself.)
Guten Tag. Ich bin Regina Janssen.

(Say where you are from and ask where she is from.)
Ich komme aus Hamburg. Ich bin auf Geschäftsreise.

Ich bin auf Geschäftsreise. *I'm on a business trip.*

Now listen to the numbers 11–20.

Numbers 11-20

11 elf		**14** vierzehn		**17** siebzehn		**19** neunzehn	
12 zwölf		**15** fünfzehn		**18** achtzehn		**20** zwanzig	
13 dreizehn		**16** sechzehn					

5. *Listen to the recording and do the sums. Then write down the sums in words and in figures.*

Example: Vierzehn plus zwei ist sechzehn. 14 + 2 = 16

6. **Kommen** *"to come" takes the regular verb endings in the present tense. Can you fill in the endings?*

ich komm _____

wir komm _____

Sie komm _____

er/sie/es komm _____

sie *(plural)* komm _____

Refer back to **heißen** *in "Close-up" on page 8 if you're not sure of the endings yet.*

Pronunciation

Now do the pronunciation exercises on the recording. Here's a table summarizing the long and short vowels:

	Short		Long	
a	kann	"can"	Tag	"day"
e	nett	"nice"	geht*	"goes"
i	ist	"is"	wie*	"how"
o	kommt	"comes"	so	"so"
u	plus	"plus"	gut	"good"

* *In some words, the long vowels are spelled* **ah; eh; ie(h); oh; uh.**

Close up

The verb **sein** *"to be"*

As in English, this is an irregular verb. It's also a very useful verb—you won't get far without learning it! Here are the forms of the present tense:

ich....................bin	I........................am
wir...................sind	we......................are
Sie ....sind	you.....................are
er/sie/es ....ist	he/she/it...............is
sie....................sind	they....................are

Checkpoints

Use this section to test everything you've learned during this unit and review anything you're unsure of.

Can you ... ?

	Yes	No
• *greet someone in the morning, afternoon, and evening*	☐	☐

Guten Morgen!
Guten Tag!
Guten Abend!

	Yes	No
• *say goodbye to someone*	☐	☐

(Auf) Wiedersehen!
Tschüs!

• *say good night*	☐	☐

Gute Nacht!

• *introduce yourself*	☐	☐

Ich heiße ...

• *ask how someone is*	☐	☐

Wie geht es Ihnen?
Wie geht's?

• *recite the alphabet*	☐	☐

A, B, C, D ...

• *spell your name*	☐	☐

...

• *count from 0 to 20*	☐	☐

Null, eins, zwei, ...

• *give your phone number*	☐	☐

...

• *ask whether you are speaking to a certain person*	☐	☐

Sind Sie Herr Schulz?

• *ask for someone to phone you back*	☐	☐

Kann er/sie mich zurückrufen?

• *ask where someone comes from*	☐	☐

Woher kommen Sie?

Can you...?	Yes	No
• *say where you come from*	☐	☐
Ich komme aus...		
• *introduce a friend*	☐	☐
Das ist...		
• *say that you are on a business trip or on vacation*	☐	☐
Ich bin auf Geschäftsreise/im Urlaub.		
• *do simple arithmetic*	☐	☐
Zwei plus vier ist sechs.		

Learning tips

Don't try to do too much at one time. It is generally better to study for short periods every day and review often than to try to do a whole unit at one sitting. Try to fix a regular time to study: find the best time of day, and always study at that time.

Do you want to learn more?

Do you have access to German-language newspapers or magazines? If so, turn to the foreign news section, and see how many country names you can recognize. If you don't have easy access to German language publications, the German, Austrian, or Swiss consulates, the national tourist offices, or the Goethe Institut may be able to help you.

For more practice, see Extra! on page A1.

Unit **2** is about buying food and drink. By the end, you'll know how to:

- order food and drink
- ask to pay, and make other requests when eating out
- ask for food items in stores and at the market
- ask how much something costs
- ask about availability of items

Was darf es sein?

2

Word Bank

alles	*everything*	der Kaffee	*coffee*
das Bier	*beer*	das Käsebrot	*cheese sandwich or roll*
bitte	*please*		
Bitte schön?	*Yes, please? (i.e., what would you like?)*	klein	*small*
		mit	*with*
die Bratwurst	*German grilled sausage*	die Pommes (frites) *(pl.)*	*French fries*
das Brot	*bread*	die Portion	*portion*
die Cola	*cola*	das Salamibrot	*salami sandwich on roll*
die Currywurst	*curried sausage*		
der Euro	*euro*	der Senf	*mustard*
groß	*big*	(Sonst) noch etwas?	*Anything else?*
ich möchte	*I would like*		
der Imbiss	*snack bar*		

Eine Portion Pommes, bitte

Buying fast food; prices; numbers 20-100

RECORDING

1. *Listen to the recording, then fill in the gaps missing in the conversation with words from the box.*

Vendor:	_____ schön?
Customer:	Ich _____ eine _____ mit Brot.
Vendor:	_____ noch etwas?
Customer:	Ja, _____ _____.
Vendor:	Noch etwas?
Customer:	Nein, _____.

bitte	Bratwurst
danke	eine Cola
möchte	sonst

RECORDING

2. *You're ordering a meal for yourself and a friend from the menu below. Listen to the recording and look at the dialogue on the next page. Follow the instructions and order from the menu below.*

SCHNELLIMBISS AM ZOO

Cola 2,50

Bratwurst mit Brot 2,50

Salamibrot 2,00

Currywurst 3,00

Bier, klein 1,90

Pommes frites 1,70

Bier, groß 2,50

Käsebrot 2,80

Kaffee 1,70

Ich möchte eine und eine .

Ja, eine Portion .

Noch etwas?

Nein, danke. Das ist alles.

Das ist alles.   *That's all.*

Now listen to the following numbers.

N u m b e r s   1 0 – 1 0 0

10 zehn	**40** vierzig	**70** siebzig	**90** neunzig
20 zwanzig	**50** fünfzig	**80** achtzig	**100** hundert
30 dreißig	**60** sechzig		

3.   *Circle the prices that you hear.*

1. 20,01; 1,20; 12,–   *6.* 30,10; 13,13; 13,10

2. 3,15; 50,03; 3,50   *7.* 50,40; 40,50; 14,15

3. 18,–; 80,–; 8,–   *8.* 7,10; 70,–; 17,–

4. 8,–; 18,–; 80,–   *9.* 7,70; 17,70; 70,70

5. 30,–; 13,–; 20,–   *10.* 9,90; 90,09; 9,10

Now read aloud the prices that you have circled.

4. *Look again at the menu on page 18. Use the prices given to identify the item ordered by each customer. Fill in the gaps below.*

> **Vendor:** Bitte schön?
> **Customer 1:** _____, bitte.
> **Vendor:** Drei Euro, bitte.
>
> **Vendor:** Bitte schön?
> **Customer 2:** _____, bitte.
> **Vendor:** Ein Euro neunzig, bitte.
>
> **Vendor:** Bitte schön?
> **Customer 3:** _____, bitte.
> **Vendor:** Zwei Euro achtzig, bitte.
>
> **Vendor:** Bitte schön?
> **Customer 4:** _____, bitte.
> **Vendor:** Zwei Euro fünfzig, bitte.

Close-up

Nouns—gender

Nouns in German have one of three underlined genders: masculine, feminine or neuter. The words for "the" and "a" (the articles) change according to the gender of the noun. For example:

	definite article "the"	indefinite article "a"
Masculine:	der Kaffee	ein Kaffee
Feminine:	die Wurst	eine Wurst
Neuter:	das Brot	ein Brot

*Note that the definite article is **die** for all nouns in the plural, regardless of gender: **die Pommes frites. Ein(e)** "a" has no direct plural.*

*There is no particular logic as to whether a noun is masculine, feminine, or neuter—although there are some clues that we'll be looking at later. You simply have to learn the gender with the noun. For this reason, it's best to learn the noun with its definite article: not **Brot** but **das Brot**. From now on, all the nouns in the Word Bank will be shown with their definite article.*

Don't worry too much if you can't remember the correct article at first!

Ein Bier, bitte!

Ordering drinks in a café

1. *Listen to the introduction on the recording, then match the most appropriate caption to each of the pictures below:*

A. Entschuldigung! Die Speisekarte bitte!

B. Was darf es sein?

C. Ich möchte bitte bestellen!

D. Ich möchte bitte bezahlen!

2.

Listen to the dialogues. Then, look at the menu, and write down what each customer orders.

Apfelschorle
apple juice and mineral water

Berliner Weiße
light beer with red or green syrup

Export
Export—a darker, fuller-bodied beer

Mit Milch oder mit Zitrone?
With milk or with lemon?

Pils
Pilsener—a light-colored beer with a dry, bitter taste

* Note that German uses a comma, not a period, to denote a decimal point. So "zero point three" is **null Komma drei.**

Zum Alten Fritz

Biere

Berliner Pils	0,3*	2,00
	0,4	2,80
Berliner Export	0,33	2,20
Berliner Weiße	0,33	2,40

Getränke–kalt

Cola	2,00
Mineralwasser	1,80
Mineralwasser, still	1,80
Orangensaft	1,90
Grapefruitsaft	2,00
Apfelsaft	2,00
Apfelschorle	2,40

Getränke–heiß

Cappuccino		2,40
Espresso		1,80
Filterkaffee	Tasse	2,00
	Kännchen	3,00
Tee (Ceylon, Earl Grey)		
	Glas	2,00
Schokolade m. Sahne		2,50

W o r d   B a n k

also	well	die Milch	milk
der Apfelsaft	apple juice	oder	or
die Bedienung	service, waitress	der Orangensaft	orange juice
bestellen	to order	das Pils	Pilsener beer
der Cappuccino	cappuccino	die Rechnung	check (bill)
der Espresso	espresso	die Sahne	cream
das Export	Export beer	die Sahnehaube	head of cream
der Fruchtsaft	fruit juice	die Schokolade	chocolate
für	for	die Speisekarte	menu
das Glas	glass	still (ohne Kohlensäure)	non-carbonated
der Grapefruitsaft	grapefruit juice	der Tee	tea
heiß	hot	was	what
Herr Ober!	Waiter!	wünschen	want, wish
der Kaffee	coffee	(be)zahlen	pay
kalt	cold	die Zitrone	lemon
das Kännchen	pot (of tea or coffee)		

3. *Play the recording. When prompted, order:*

    a. a tea

    b. a coffee

    c. a beer

    d. an orange juice

4. *Listen to the recording, and look at the checks below.*
Which check belongs to which table?

Zum Alten Fritz Dahlemer Straße 415 13410 Berlin	
2 kleine Pils	2,00
	2,00
1 Cappuccino	2,40
1 Apfelschorle	2,40
	8,80

Zum Alten Fritz Dahlemer Straße 415 13410 Berlin	
2 Glas Tee	2,00
	2,00
1 Kännchen	
Filterkaffee	3,00
	7,00

Zum Alten Fritz Dahlemer Straße 415 13410 Berlin	
1 Mineralwasser,	
still	1,80
1 Espresso	1,80
	3,60

    a.   b.   c.

Ich hätte gern . . .
Ich möchte . . . } *I would like . . .*

Wir hätten gern . . .
Wir möchten . . . } *We would like . . .*

Close-up

Masculine nouns

On page 20 we said that it's **ein Kaffee**. So why do we say **Ich möchte einen Kaffee**?

To understand this, you need to know a little about _subjects_ and _objects_. When you say **Ich möchte einen Kaffee,** you are the subject, the one who _wants_ the coffee. The coffee is the object, the thing that _is wanted_. To put it another way, the subject is performing the action; the object is affected by the action. So in the sentence "Man bites dog," the man is the subject, the one who performs the action; the dog is the object, the one who is affected.

Now, when a masculine noun becomes the object of a verb, **ein** can change to **einen**. Only the masculine articles change in this way:

Masculine:	ein Kaffee:	Ich möchte einen Kaffee.
Feminine:	eine Cola:	Ich möchte eine Cola.
Neuter:	ein Brot:	Ich möchte ein Brot.

Don't worry if you get it wrong: you'll still be understood!

Zwei Euro das Kilo

Buying produce at the market

1. *Which conversation belongs to each of these market stalls?*

a. Obst & Gemüse

Käthes Blumen

b. Souvenirs 3,70

Käse

c. Bäckerei Moritz

e.

d.

Sie duften so gut!	*They smell so nice!*
Es schmeckt gut!	*It tastes good!*
Was kostet es?	*How much is it?*
Sehen Sie?	*You see?*
Vier Stück, bitte.	*Four, please. (Literally: Four pieces, please.)*

Word Bank

aber	*but*	kosten	*to cost*
die Ansichtskarte (-n)	*postcard*	lecker	*delicious*
die Bäckerei (-en)	*bakery*	nehmen	*to take*
billig	*cheap*	die Nelke (-n)	*carnation*
bitte schön	*here you are*	das Obst	*fruit*
dann	*then, in that case*	die Olive (-n)	*olive*
diese	*these*	die Orange (-n)	*orange*
ganz	*very; completely*	probieren	*to try*
das Gemüse	*vegetable(s)*	die Rose (-n)	*rose*
das Gramm (-)	*gram*	der Schafskäse	*sheep's milk cheese*
groß	*big*	schwarz	*black*
haben	*to have*	das Souvenir (-s)	*souvenir*
insgesamt	*altogether*	süß	*sweet*
der Käse	*cheese*	das Vollkornbrot (-e)	*whole wheat bread*

Listen to the recording and practice the shopping language before continuing with Activity 2.

Did You Know?

*I*n 2002 the euro (**der Euro**) became the official currency in Germany and Austria, replacing the Deutschmark and the Austrian shilling.

One euro equals 100 cent.

The Swiss currency is the Swiss franc (**der Schweizer Franken**) abbreviated **sFr**. One franc equals 100 **Rappen**.

German-speaking countries only use the metric

2. *You're going shopping at the market. Here's your list of things to buy:*

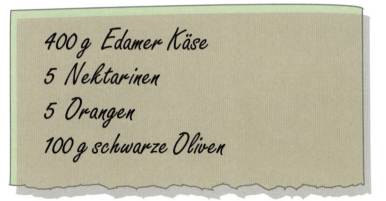

400 g Edamer Käse
5 Nektarinen
5 Orangen
100 g schwarze Oliven

To get you started, here's the first dialogue, with space for you to complete your responses:

Vendor: Guten Tag! Sie wünschen?

You: *(Say hello, ask if he has Edam cheese)*
_____ _____ . Haben Sie _____ _____ ?

Vendor: Aber natürlich! Hundert Gramm für neunzig Cent.

You: *(You'll take four hundred grams.)*
Ich nehme _____ _____ .

Vendor: Bitte schön. Sonst noch etwas?

You: *(No, thanks.)* _____ , _____ .

Vendor: Drei Euro sechzig, bitte.

Try to make the remaining purchases without preparing written notes.

Darf ich probieren?   *May I try (taste)?*

3. *Here are the numbers 20–24. Can you complete writing the numbers up to forty? The pattern is completely regular.*

20 zwanzig	**27**	**34**
21 einundzwanzig	**28**	**35**
22 zweiundzwanzig	**29**	**36**
23 dreiundzwanzig	**30**	**37**
24 vierundzwanzig	**31**	**38**
25	**32**	**39**
26	**33**	**40**

4. *Circle the number you hear from each pair:*

a. 34 43		f. 62 26
b. 13 30		g. 39 93
c. 97 79		h. 80 18
d. 35 53		i. 41 51
e. 82 28		j. 56 65

Pronunciation

How would you pronounce these words?

Tag	*day*	**Käse**	*cheese*
schon	*already*	**schön**	*beautiful*
gut	*good*	**Stück**	*piece*

Now do the pronunciation practice on the recording.

Numbers 100-1000

100	(ein)hundert	**500**	fünfhundert	**900**	neunhundert
200	zweihundert	**600**	sechshundert	**1000**	tausend
300	dreihundert	**700**	siebenhundert		
400	vierhundert	**800**	achthundert		

Close up

Nouns—plural

Not many German nouns form their plurals with an **-s** *like English
nouns (these are usually words taken from English and French:
e.g.* **das Souvenir**, **die Souvenirs**). *Feminine nouns ending in* **-
e** *in the singular always take* **-n** *in the plural:*

die Rose	the rose
die Rosen	the roses

*You'll come across other plural forms in the following units. The
plural ending will be shown in the Word Bank, in parentheses
after the noun. (-) means that the noun doesn't change in the plural.*

Checkpoints

Use this section to test everything you've learned during this unit and review anything you're unsure of.

Can you...?

	Yes	No
• *attract the waiter or waitress' attention*	☐	☐

Hallo!
Entschuldigung!

	Yes	No
• *ask to order*	☐	☐

Ich möchte bitte bestellen.

	Yes	No
• *ask for the menu*	☐	☐

Die Speisekarte, bitte!

	Yes	No
• *order food and drink in a café or snack bar*	☐	☐

Ich möchte/hätte gern eine Bratwurst.
Eine Bratwurst, bitte.
Ich möchte/hätte gern einen Kaffee.
Einen Kaffee, bitte.
Ich möchte/hätte gern ein großes Bier.
Ein großes Bier, bitte.

	Yes	No
• *say that's all*	☐	☐

Das ist alles.

	Yes	No
• *ask to pay*	☐	☐

Ich möchte bitte bezahlen.

	Yes	No
• *count from 21 to 99*	☐	☐

Einundzwanzig, zweiundzwanzig... neunundneunzig.

	Yes	No
• *count from 100 to 1000*	☐	☐

Hundert, zweihundert... tausend.

	Yes	No
• *ask about availability of an item*	☐	☐

Haben Sie Fruchtsaft?
Haben Sie Käse?

	Yes	No
• *ask for a specific weight of an item*	☐	☐

Vierhundert Gramm Käse, bitte.

Can you...?	Yes	No
• *ask about price*	☐	☐

Was kostet es?
Was kosten sie?

| • *ask to taste something* .... | ☐ | ☐ |

Darf ich probieren?

Learning tips

Be selective in your vocabulary learning. Don't feel that you have to learn every word and expression you find in this course. Instead, choose the 15–20 words or expressions from each spread that seem most useful and relevant to you, and aim to make them stick in your memory. That way, by the end of the course you'll have an active German vocabulary of between 540 and 720 words. But you'll also find that you've absorbed a much larger passive vocabulary through hearing and reading lots of German.

Do you want to learn more?

If someone you know is going to a German-speaking country, ask them to bring back magazines with cooking recipes, and checks from restaurants and cafés. Some restaurants and cafés may let you take a menu. See how many names of foods and drinks you can identify, and practice ordering them.

For more practice, see Extra! on page A4.

SPARKASSE

U nit 3 is about exchanging personal information with people you meet. By the end, you'll know how to:

- state your marital status
- list your family members
- say what you do for a living
- state your nationality
- say what languages you speak

Alles über mich

3

Word Bank

aber	*but*	das Kind (-er)	*child*
der Bruder (¨)	*brother*	klein	*small*
die Eltern	*parents*	leben	*to live*
das Enkelkind (-er)	*grandchild*	ledig	*single, unmarried*
der Enkelsohn (-söhne)	*grandson*	leider	*unfortunately*
die Enkeltochter (-töchter)	*granddaughter*	der Mann (¨-er)	*husband; man*
die Familie (-n)	*family*	mein/e	*my*
die Frau (-en)	*wife; Mrs.; woman*	die Mutter (¨)	*mother*
geschieden	*divorced*	noch	*still*
die Geschwister	*brothers and sisters, siblings*	noch nicht	*not yet*
getrennt	*separated*	der Partner (-)	*partner (male)*
die Großmutter (-mütter)	*grandmother*	die Partnerin (-nen)	*partner (female)*
der Großvater (-väter)	*grandfather*	die Schwester (-n)	*sister*
haben	*to have*	der Sohn (¨-e)	*son*
Ihr/e	*your*	die Tochter (¨)	*daughter*
jung	*young*	der Vater (¨)	*father*
kein/e	*none, not any*	verheiratet	*married*
		zu	*too; to*

Das ist meine Familie

Talking about the family

1. *Put these sentences in the order in which they occur on the recording. Then write down what you think they mean in English. You'll find any new words in the Word Bank. We've filled in the first one for you.*

a. Ja, aber wir leben getrennt. <u>*Yes, but we're separated*</u>
   <u>*(or: we live apart.)*</u>

b. Nein, ich bin noch ledig.

c. Ja, ich bin verheiratet.

d. Nein, aber ich habe einen Partner.

e. Nein, ich bin geschieden.

2. *Listen to six different speakers. How many sons and daughters does each have?*

Haben Sie Kinder?	*Do you have children?*
Ich bin also Großmutter.	*So I'm a grandmother.*
Nein, noch nicht.	*No, not yet.*

3. *Fill in the family tree with the words for relatives from the box.*

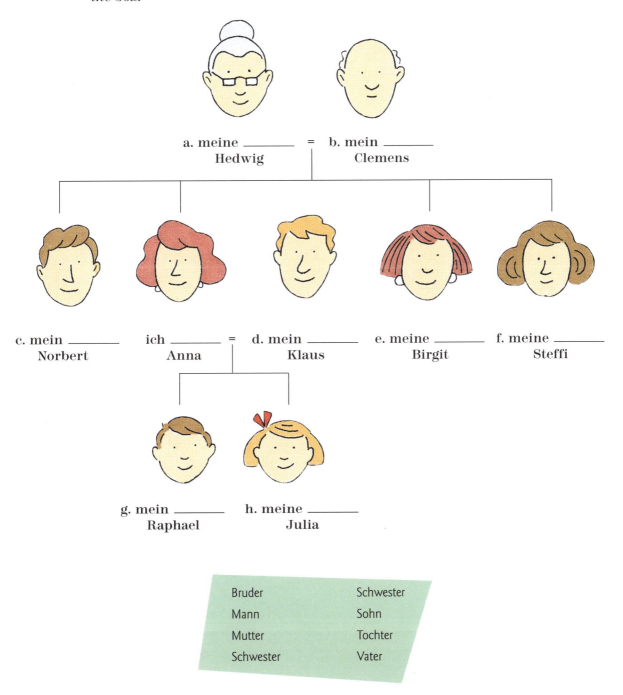

a. meine _____   =   b. mein _____
    Hedwig   Clemens

c. mein _____   ich _____ = d. mein _____   e. meine _____   f. meine _____
  Norbert   Anna   Klaus   Birgit   Steffi

g. mein _____   h. meine _____
  Raphael   Julia

Bruder	Schwester
Mann	Sohn
Mutter	Tochter
Schwester	Vater

Haben Sie Geschwister?　　*Do you have brothers and sisters?*

4. *Answer these questions about the members of Frau Wieland's family. Use **ihr/ihre,** "her," instead of **Frau Wieland,** as in the example. Note that you have to use **ihr** for masculine and **ihre** for feminine family members.*

Example: Heißt Frau Wielands Bruder Richard?
<u>Nein, ihr Bruder heißt Norbert.</u>

a. Heißen Frau Wielands Eltern Julia und Raphael?

b. Heißen Frau Wielands Schwestern Anna und Steffi?

c. Wie heißt Frau Wielands Tochter?

d. Heißt Frau Wielands Mann Klaus?

e. Heißt Frau Wielands Sohn Norbert?

5. **Sie sind dran!** *It's your turn! You're going to ask Herr Fromm these questions. Prepare some written notes to help you before playing the recording.*

a. *Are you married?*

b. *What is your wife called?*

c. *Do you have any brothers or sisters (**Geschwister**)?*

d. *Do you have children?*

Nein, ich habe keine Geschwister.
No, I don't have any brothers or sisters.

Close up

Verbs: **haben** "to have"

Haben is an irregular verb. You'll need it often, so it's worth memorizing:

ich	habe	I	have
wir	haben	we	have
Sie	haben	you	have
er/sie/es	hat	he/she/it	has
sie	haben	they	have

Nominative and accusative cases

Remember what we said about subjects and objects. In the sentence: **Ich habe einen Bruder**, "I have a brother," **ich** is the subject, the one who "has"; **Bruder** is the object, the one who is "had," and so it's **einen Bruder**. (The <u>subject</u> of a sentence is said to be "in the <u>nominative</u> case" and the <u>object</u> is here "in the <u>accusative</u> case.")

Possessive adjectives

The possessive adjectives are: **mein** "my," **unser** "our," **Ihr** "your," **sein** "his, its," and **ihr** "her, their." They take the same endings as the indefinite article **ein**:

Das ist mein/unser/Ihr/sein/ihr Bruder.

Das ist mein<u>e</u>/unser<u>e</u>/Ihr<u>e</u>/sein<u>e</u>/ihr<u>e</u> Schwester.

Das ist mein/unser/Ihr/sein/ihr Kind.

If they refer to a plural noun, they take the ending **-e**:

Das sind mein<u>e</u>/unser<u>e</u>/Ihr<u>e</u>/sein<u>e</u>/ihr<u>e</u> Brüder (Schwestern/Kinder).

Not any: **kein**

Kein is the negative of **ein**, as in **Ich habe keinen Bruder**, "I don't have a brother." (*Ich habe nicht einen Bruder* is incorrect German.) **Kein** takes the same endings as the possessive adjectives above.

Was sind Sie von Beruf?

Saying what you do for a living

Word Bank

an	*at*	in	*in*
arbeiten	*to work*	das Krankenhaus (-häuser)	*hospital*
arbeitslos	*unemployed*	das Restaurant (-s)	*restaurant*
die Bank (-en)	*bank*	die Schule (-n)	*school*
bei	*at; for (e.g., work for a company)*	selbständig	*independent(ly), for oneself*
der Beruf (-e)	*profession*	die Universität (-en)	*university*
das Büro (-s)	*office*	wahr	*true*
die Fabrik (-en)	*factory*	Was sind Sie von Beruf?	*What's your profession?*
falsch	*false*	wo	*where*
Geschäft	*store; business*	zur Zeit	*at the moment*

1. *Listen to the recording. You will hear five people giving their name and their profession. Fill in their professions on the business cards below. You might refer to the list of professions on page 40.*

Berufe—*Professions*

Don't attempt to learn all these professions. Do notice that the feminine forms are usually formed by adding -in to the masculine forms.

masculine	feminine	
Architekt (-en)	Architektin (-nen)	*architect*
Arzt ("-e)	Ärztin (-nen)	*doctor*
Bauarbeiter (-)	Bauarbeiterin (-nen)	*construction worker*
Fotograf (-en)	Fotografin (-nen)	*photographer*
Friseur (-e)	Friseuse (-n)	*hairdresser*
Kassierer (-)	Kassiererin (-nen)	*cashier*
Kellner (-)	Kellnerin (-nen)	*waiter, waitress*
Krankenpfleger (-)	Krankenpflegerin (-nen)	*nurse*
Kundenberater (-)	Kundenberaterin (-nen)	*customer adviser*
Künstler (-)	Künstlerin (-nen)	*artist*
Lehrer (-)	Lehrerin (-nen)	*teacher*
Professor (-en)	Professorin (-nen)	*professor*
Regisseur (-e)	Regisseurin (-nen)	*(film) director*
Rennfahrer (-)	Rennfahrerin (-nen)	*racing driver*
Schauspieler (-)	Schauspielerin (-nen)	*actor, actress*
Student (-en)	Studentin (-nen)	*student*
Taxifahrer (-)	Taxifahrerin (-nen)	*taxi driver*
Techniker (-)	Technikerin (-nen)	*technician*
Verkäufer (-)	Verkäuferin (-nen)	*sales clerk*

Did You Know?

Over 100 million people speak German as their native language. The majority live in Germany, Austria, and the German-speaking part of Switzerland, but there are also German-speaking areas of Italy (South Tyrol), France (Alsace), Luxembourg, Belgium, parts of Eastern Europe, and Russia, as well as German-speaking communities in North and South America and in eastern and southern Africa (e.g., Namibia).

There are more than 40 different dialects of German. Some of the main ones are: **Plattdeutsch** *(northern Germany);* **Sächsisch** *(parts of eastern Germany);* **Bayerisch** *(Bavaria) and the closely related* **Österreichisch** *(Austria);* **Schwäbisch** *(south central Germany); and* **Alemannisch** *(spoken in southwestern Germany and parts of Switzerland—the Swiss version is commonly called* **Schwyzerdütsch** *or* **Schweizerdeutsch***).*

2. *What are the professions of the people below? Write down what they do for a living. Make also negative statements.*

Dieter Speck

Sonja Brückner

Rudi Dessau

Andreas Freitag

a. Dieter Speck ist _____ . Er ist nicht _____ .

b. Sonja Brückner ist _____ . Sie ist nicht _____ .

c. Rudi Dessau ist _____ . Er ist nicht _____ .

d. Andreas Freitag ist _____ . Er ist nicht _____ .

Bauarbeiter	Künstler	Schauspielerin
Friseuse	Regisseur	Taxifahrer
Kassierer	Rennfahrer	

3. *Listen to the speakers saying where they work. Then decide which of these statements fits each person.*

a. Ich bin Kassiererin.

b. Ich bin Kellner.

c. Ich bin Krankenpfleger.

d. Ich bin Lehrerin.

e. Ich bin Professorin.

f. Ich bin Verkäufer.

4. *When you're asked whether you work in a place, say* **Ja, ich bin...** *and give a suitable job title, remembering to use the male or female form as appropriate. Here are the questions; you might want to prepare your answers before listening to the recording.*

a. Arbeiten Sie in einem Restaurant?

b. Arbeiten Sie in einem Geschäft?

c. Arbeiten Sie in einer Schule?

d. Arbeiten Sie an der Universität?

e. Arbeiten Sie in einer Bank?

f. Arbeiten Sie in einem Krankenhaus?

Now say where you really work, and what your real job title is.

Close up

Dative case

Notice that the German for "in a bank" is **in einer Bank**, *and "in a store" is* **in einem Geschäft**. *These are the endings of the* <u>dative</u> *case. The dative is used after prepositions (words that indicate position) like* **in** *"in," or* **an** *"at," when they indicate location, and always after the prepositions* **aus** *"out of/from" and* **von** *"from/of."*

Sie sprechen gut Deutsch!

Talking about languages and nationalities

1. ***Which of these languages do you hear mentioned on the recording? Write down their English translations.***

Deutsch   Polnisch

Englisch   Russisch

Französisch   Spanisch

Italienisch   Türkisch

Word Bank

alt	old	das Land (¨-er)	country
das Alter	age	die Muttersprache (-n)	native language, mother tongue
außerdem	also	die Postleitzahl (-en)	zip code
Deutsch	German		
Englisch	English	die Schweiz	Switzerland
etwas	a bit; something	sprechen	speak
der Familienstand	marital status	die Staatsangehörigkeit (-en)	nationality
Französisch	French	die Straße (-n)	street, road
die Fremdsprache (-n)	foreign language	die Türkei	Turkey
genauso	just as	wie	as; how
das Jahr (-e)	year	wohnen	live
jetzt	now	der Wohnort (-e)	place of residence (town)

2. *Look at the nationalities in the box: who speaks each of the languages listed under Activity 1? Be careful: some languages are spoken in more than one country—and in some countries, more than one language is spoken.*

Amerikaner/in	Italiener/in	Russe/Russin
Australier/in	Kanadier/in	Schweizer/in
Brite/Britin	Österreicher/in	Spanier/in
Deutscher/Deutsche	Pole/Polin	Türke/Türkin
Franzose/Französin		

3. *These application forms were sent to a language school by prospective teachers. Listen to the recording, then fill in the missing details.*

Name: Berger	Vorname: Claudia
Straße, Nr.: Mozartstraße 72	
PLZ: A 8 0 1 0	**Wohnort:** Graz
Land:	
Staatsangehörigkeit: österreichisch	
Muttersprache:	
Fremdsprachen:	
Alter:	
Familienstand	

a.

Name: Dogan	Vorname: Mustafa
Straße, Nr.: Domstraße 90	
PLZ: 7 9 0 9 8	**Wohnort:** Freiburg
Land: Deutschland	
Staatsangehörigkeit:	
Muttersprache: / Deutsch	
Fremdsprachen: , Italienisch	
Alter:	
Familienstand verheiratet	

b.

Name: Tschumi	Vorname: Hans
Straße, Nr.: Spandauer Straße 110a	
PLZ: 1 0 7 8 3	**Wohnort:** Berlin
Land:	
Staatsangehörigkeit:	
Muttersprache: Deutsch	
Fremdsprachen: ,	
Alter: 31	
Familienstand	

c.

etwas Italienisch	a bit of Italian
genauso gut wie	just as well as
Ich bin... Jahre alt.	I'm... years old.
Ich wohne jetzt in Berlin.	I live in Berlin now.
Nr. = Nummer	number
PLZ = Postleitzahl	zip code

4. **Sie sind dran!** *Write out a form for yourself.*

Before continuing with Activity 5, you may want to listen to the recording again to find out how to say where you live and where you are from.

5. **Sie sind dran!** *Practice introducing yourself the way the speakers did on the recording. Remember to state:*

a. your name	(Ich heiße...)
b. your nationality	(Ich bin...)
c. the town and the country you live in	(Ich komme aus/wohne in...)
d. what languages you speak	(Ich spreche...)
e. your age	(Ich bin... Jahre alt)
f. your marital status	(Ich bin...)

Pronunciation

Let's practice some pronounciation now. Listen to the recording.

Close-up

Verbs: **sprechen** *"to speak"*

ich	spreche	I	speak
wir	sprechen	we	speak
Sie	sprechen	you (formal)	speak
er/sie/es	<u>spricht</u>	he/she/it	speaks
sie	sprechen	they	speak

If a verb is irregular in the present tense, it's usually only irregular in the **er/sie/es** *form. From now on, we'll just be giving you the irregular forms in the Word Bank; we won't be showing the whole verb in Close-up.*

Nationalities: feminine forms

The feminine forms of nationalities are generally very easy to form. Like the feminine forms of professions, they add the ending **-in** *to the masculine form:* **Schweizer/Schweizerin** *"Swiss man/woman," etc. Watch out for these irregular ones:*

Brite/Britin	*British man/woman*
Deutscher/Deutsche	*German man/woman*
Franzose/Französin	*French man/woman*
Pole/Polin	*Polish man/woman*
Russe/Russin	*Russian man/woman*
Türke/Türkin	*Turkish man/woman*

Checkpoints

Use this section to test everything you've learned during this unit and review anything you're unsure of.

Can you ... ?

	Yes	No
• *state your marital status*	☐	☐

Ich bin verheiratet.
Ich bin ledig.
Ich bin geschieden.

• *ask someone about their marital status*	☐	☐

Sind Sie verheiratet?

• *list the members of your family*	☐	☐

Ich habe einen Bruder.
Ich habe eine Schwester.
Ich habe einen Sohn.
Ich habe eine Tochter.
Ich habe einen Partner.
Ich habe eine Partnerin.

• *give the names of family members*	☐	☐

Mein Vater heißt...
Meine Mutter heißt...

• *ask someone about their family*	☐	☐

Haben Sie Familie?
Wie heißt Ihr Sohn?

• *say what you and others do for a living*	☐	☐

Ich bin Architekt/in.
Er ist Taxifahrer.
Sie ist Kassiererin.
Sie sind arbeitslos.

• *say where you work*	☐	☐

Ich arbeite in einer Bank/an einer Universität/bei Mercedes.

• *say what languages you speak*	☐	☐

Ich spreche Deutsch/Englisch/Französisch.

Can you...?   **Yes**   **No**

- *give your nationality* . . . . ☐ . . . . . ☐
  Ich bin Amerikaner/in.
  Ich bin Brite/Britin.
  Ich bin Deutscher/Deutsche.
  Ich bin Schweizer/Schweizerin.
  Ich bin Österreicher/Österreicherin

- *state your age* . . . . ☐ . . . . . ☐
  Ich bin... Jahre alt.

Learning tips

*Try recording your voice when you speak, and listen to the
recording to see how you might be able to improve. Record your
voice regularly, and keep the recordings. Go back to the
beginning of your recording after a few weeks or months to see
how you have improved!*

Do you want to learn more?

*Turn to the employment advertisements in a German-language
newspaper to see how many of the jobs you recognize. Use clues
from the name of the company. Guess what the job title might
mean, and then check with your dictionary.*

For more practice, see Extra! on page A6.

U nit 4 will introduce you to some language for checking into a hotel and finding your way around town. By the end, you'll know how to:

- ask about facilities and prices
- check into a hotel
- ask for directions
- state the time and the day
- ask about opening times

Willkommen in Berlin!

4

Word Bank

ab+reisen	*to leave, depart*	das Frühstück	*breakfast*
alles	*all, everything*	heute	*today*
das Anmeldeformular (-e)	*registration form*	inklusive	*included; inclusive*
die Anschrift (-en)	*address*	der Moment (-e)	*moment*
aus+füllen	*to fill out*	die Nacht (¨-e)	*night*
die Ausweisnummer (-n)	*ID number, passport number*	nehmen	*to take*
das Bad (¨-er)	*bath*	oje	*oh dear*
belegt	*occupied, taken*	die Person (-en)	*person*
bestellen	*to reserve, order*	pro	*per*
bleiben	*to stay*	teuer	*expensive*
das Doppelzimmer (-)	*double room*	das WC (-s)	*WC; toilet*
die Dusche (-n)	*shower*	wenigstens	*at least*
das Einzelzimmer (-)	*single room*	Wie lange?	*How long?*
extra	*extra*	willkommen	*welcome*
das Formular (-e)	*form*	die Woche (-n)	*week*
frei	*free, vacant*	das Zimmer (-)	*room*

Ein Doppelzimmer mit Dusche

Booking a hotel room

1. *Who's staying where? Match the names with the room numbers. Careful: there are two numbers too many.*

117

119   a. Herr Bachmann

123   b. Frau Armbruster

132   c. Herr Bader

217   d. Frau Reisner

219

One of the guests is checking out: who is it?

Ich habe ein Zimmer bestellt.	*I've reserved a room.*
Füllen Sie bitte das Formular aus.	*Fill out the form, please.*
Ich reise heute ab.	*I'm leaving today.*

2. *Can you write out the numbers in words? We've done the first two for you, and the pattern is completely regular, but remember to put the units before the tens.*

101   (ein)hunderteins

121   hunderteinundzwanzig

201

221

199

257

375

999

3.

Complete the details of the three hotels.

	Hotel 1	Hotel 2	Hotel 3
Einzelzimmer pro Nacht	80,–	_____,–	_____,–
Doppelzimmer pro Nacht	_____,–	75,–	_____,–
mit WC	_____	ja	
mit Dusche/Bad	_____	_____	
mit Frühstück	_____	_____	nein

Ist das ein Zimmer mit Bad?	*Is that a room with a bath?*
Alles belegt.	*All taken./No vacancy.*
Haben Sie ein Doppelzimmer frei?	*Do you have a double room free?*
Ich nehme es für eine Nacht.	*I'll take it for one night.*
Wir sind ein Hotel garni.	*This is a "hotel garni." (a hotel that provides bed and breakfast)*
Das ist zu teuer!	*That's too expensive!*

Now practice saying how long you want to stay.

4.

Sie sind dran! *You'd like a double room at the Hotel Spreewald. Write down what you're going to say first, then play the recording.*

Receptionist: Guten Abend! Kann ich etwas für Sie tun?

You: *(Ask if she has a double room available.)*

Receptionist: Wie lange möchten Sie bleiben?

You: *(Three nights.)*

Receptionist: Ja, wir haben ein Doppelzimmer frei. Das kostet neunzig Euro pro Nacht.

You: *(Is breakfast included?)*

Receptionist: Ja, Frühstück ist inklusive.

You: *(Say you'll take it.)*

5. *Fill out this hotel registration form.*

HOTEL SPREEWALD

— ■ —

Anmeldeformular

Familienname: _____

Vorname: _____

Anschrift

Straße/Nummer: _____

PLZ/Wohnort: _____

Land: _____

Ausweisnummer: _____

Close up

Separable verbs: **abreisen, ausfüllen**

Did you notice that "I'm leaving" is **ich reise ab**, *but the infinitive "to leave" is* **abreisen**? *Similarly "I fill out (a form)" is* **ich fülle (ein Formular) aus**, *but the infinitive "to fill out" is* **ausfüllen**. *These are* separable *verbs: they consist of a normal verb and a preposition. In the infinitive form, the preposition is prefixed to the verb, but when the verb is used with a subject, the preposition goes to the end of the sentence:*

aus + füllen	Ich <u>fülle</u> es <u>aus</u>.	I fill it out.
ab + reisen	Ich <u>reise</u> heute <u>ab</u>.	I leave today.

All separable verbs are marked by + between prefix and verb in the Word Bank.

Wo ist hier eine Post?

Asking for directions

Word Bank

an (+ dat.)	at		nochmal	again
die Bäckerei (-en)	bakery		die Post	post office
die Bank (-en)	bank		die Querstraße (-n)	intersection, junction
der Blumenladen (-läden)	flower shop, florist's		rechts	right
die Buchhandlung (-en)	book shop		sehen	to see
das Café (-s)	café		die Seite (-n)	side
da vorne	over there		die Straße (-n)	street, road
die Ecke (-n)	corner		der Taxistand (¨-e)	taxi stand
Entschuldigung!	Excuse me!		die Telefonzelle (-n)	phone booth
es tut mir leid	I'm sorry		die U-Bahn-Station (-en)	subway station
finden	to find		um (+ acc.)	around
der Geldautomat (-en)	ATM, cash machine		verstehen	to understand
gehen	to go		vielleicht	perhaps
geradeaus	straight ahead		vor (+ dat.)	in front of
gleich	just, immediately		war	was (infinitive: sein)
das Hotel (-s)	hotel		weiß	know (infinitive: wissen)
immer	always			
der Laden (¨)	shop, store		weiter	further
langsamer	slower, more slowly		Wie bitte?	Pardon?
leicht	easy		Wo?	Where?
links	left		der Zeitungshändler (-)	newsdealer
der Meter (-)	meter		zum (= zu dem)	to the (masculine and neuter)
neben (+ dat.)	next to			

1. *You want the following items; where would you find them? Match the items to the places in the box. (Some items can be found in more than one place.)*

die Post	das Restaurant	die Buchhandlung
der Zeitungshändler	die Bank	der Geldautomat
das Café	der Blumenladen	

2. *Insert* **eine** *or* **ein** *in the blank as appropriate:*

a. Entschuldigung, wo ist hier _____ Post?

b. Entschuldigung, wo ist hier _____ Restaurant?

c. Entschuldigung, wo ist hier _____ Café?

d. Entschuldigung, wo ist hier _____ Buchhandlung?

e. Entschuldigung, wo ist hier _____ Blumenladen?

f. Entschuldigung, wo ist hier _____ Zeitungshändler?

g. Entschuldigung, wo ist hier _____ Bank?

h. Entschuldigung, wo ist hier _____ Geldautomat?

Choose the correct diagram to illustrate each dialog.
(Some diagrams match more than one dialog.)

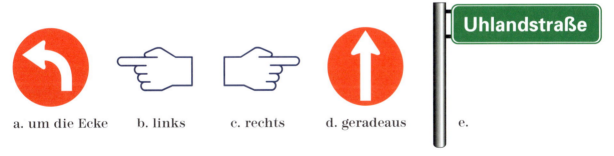

a. um die Ecke   b. links   c. rechts   d. geradeaus   e.

Match these places with the letters on the map. You can
refer to expressions on the next page for help if you like.

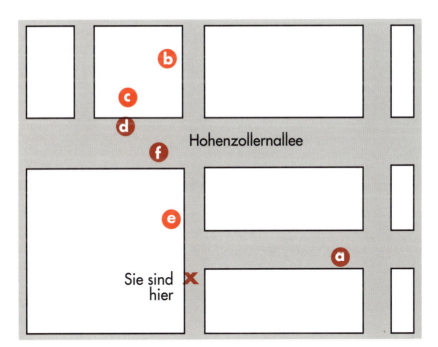

1. Hotel Spreewald   4. Bäckerei

2. Café Dreiklang   5. Taxistand

3. U-Bahn-Station Uhlandstraße   6. Telefonzelle

auf der rechten Seite
on the right

(Das ist) ganz leicht zu finden.
That's very easy to find.

(Das) weiß ich auch nicht.
I don't know that either.

(Es) tut mir leid.
I'm sorry.

Ich bin nicht von hier.
I'm not from around here.

(Ich) weiß (es) nicht.
I don't know.

Vielleicht vierhundert Meter weiter.
Maybe four hundred meters farther on.

5. *Listen now to some questions you can ask if you did not understand. Fill in the missing word.*

a. _____ bitte?

b. Wie war das noch _____?

c. _____, bitte!

d. Wie _____ die Straße?

e. _____ Sie das buchstabieren?

f. Ich verstehe _____.

Close-up

Compound nouns: gender

As you'll have noticed, German has some very long words! However, these are usually just two or more words written together (compounds). If you can recognize the components, grasping the meaning of the compound isn't usually a problem. For example:

die Blumen + der Laden = der Blumenladen

the flowers + the shop = the flower shop (literally: the "flowers shop") Compound nouns like **Blumenladen** take the gender of the last component: it's **die Blume** but **der Laden**, so it's **der Blumenladen**.

Instructions and commands: the imperative

When instructing someone to do something, you can use the imperative or command form. The verb comes at the beginning of the sentence, just like in a question:

Sie <u>gehen</u> geradeaus.	You go straight ahead. (statement)
<u>Gehen</u> Sie geradeaus?	Are you going straight ahead? (question)
<u>Gehen</u> Sie geradeaus!	Go straight ahead! (instruction)

If you address someone formally, in Geman you literally say "Go <u>you</u> straight ahead," not just "Go straight ahead," like English.

Wie viel Uhr ist es?

Time and opening times

1. **Wie viel Uhr ist es?** *What time is it? Listen to the recording first, then complete the times below.*

A. Es ist _____ Uhr.

B. Es ist _____ Uhr dreißig./Es ist halb _____.

C. Es ist _____ _____.

D. Es ist _____ Uhr fünfzehn./Es ist Viertel nach _____.

E. Es ist _____ Uhr dreißig. Es ist halb _____.

F. _____ _____ _____ _____.

G. _____ _____ _____ _____ _____./_____ _____

       _____ _____.

H. Es ist _____ _____ fünfundvierzig. Es ist _____ vor _____.

W o r d B a n k

die Bibliothek (-en)	*library*	die Nachrichten *(pl)*	*news*
bis	*to, until*	die Öffnungszeiten *(pl)*	*opening times*
die Dame (-n)	*lady*	der Ruhetag (-e)	*day off, closed day*
der Gast (¨-e)	*guest*	(die) Uhr (-en)	*clock; o'clock (in times)*
geöffnet	*open, opened*		
geschlossen	*closed*	um	*at*
halb zwei	*half past one (literally: half to two)*	Um wie viel Uhr?	*At what time?*
		Viertel nach/vor	*a quarter past/to*
der Herr (-en)	*gentleman/man*	von	*from*
lieb	*dear*	vor	*to, before*
nach	*past, after*	Wann?	*When?*
		Wie viel?	*How much?*

2. *At what times do the news bulletins occur? Use the 24-hour clock in your answers.*

liebe Hörerinnen und Hörer	*dear guests (i.e., listeners)*
um... Uhr	*at... o'clock*
Wie spät ist es?	*How late is it?*

3. *Here are the days of the week—in the proper order from Monday to Sunday, but with the letters scrambled. Can you rearrange them? Remember to begin each one with a capital letter.*

a. **gamnot** _____

b. **adeginst** _____

c. **chimottw** _____

d. **degnanorst** _____

e. **efgirat** _____

f. **gamsast/bandennos** _____

g. **gannost** _____

4. *Match the signs with the recorded messages.*

<table>
<tr><td>

Stadtmuseum

Mo	Geschlossen
Di–Sa	10–17 Uhr
So	11–17 Uhr

</td><td>

Universitäts-Bibliothek
Öffnungszeiten
——————

Mo–Mi	10.00–19.30
Do	10.00–21.00
Fr	10.00–19.30
Sa	10.00–13.00
So	Geschlossen
——————

</td><td>

**Touristen-
Information**

Mo–Fr	8.00 bis 19.00
Sa	8.00 bis 16.00
So	10.00 bis 16.00

</td></tr>
</table>

5. *You're working in your local tourist office, and a German tourist phones to ask what times you're open. Here are the times; how are you going to state them in German? Write down your answers on the following page, then play the recording.*

Monday–Friday:	9–16:00
Saturday:	9–18:00
Sunday:	closed

Tourist: Wann haben Sie montags bis freitags geöffnet?

You: Wir haben montags _____ geöffnet.

Tourist: Und Samstag?

You: Wir haben samstags _____ geöffnet.

Tourist: Und sonntags?

You: Sonntags haben wir _____.

Wann haben Sie geöffnet?   *When are you open?*

Pronunciation

How would you pronounce these words?

Wein	*(wine)*	**Wien**	*(Vienna)*
weiter	*(further)*	**wieder**	*(again)*
Reise	*(trip)*	**Riesling**	*(Riesling—a type of grape)*

Now do Pronunciation Practice on the recording.

Close up

Days of the week

To say that something happens regularly "on Mondays," "on Tuesdays," etc., add **-s** to the day of the week:

> Die Bibliothek hat montags von neun bis neunzehn Uhr geöffnet; dienstags...
>
> *The library is open on Mondays from nine A.M. to seven P.M.; on Tuesdays...*

You write **montags, dienstags,** etc., with a small letter, but you write **Montag, Dienstag,** etc. with a capital.

Word order

In German, you can change the word order for emphasis, but the verb <u>must</u> come second in the sentence. For example:

> Montags <u>hat</u> die Bibliothek von neun bis neunzehn Uhr geöffnet.
>
> *On Mondays, the library <u>is</u> open from nine A.M. to seven P.M.*

DidYouKnow?

On November 1, 1996, Bundestag-enacted legislation went into effect modestly liberalizing German business hours.

Stores and shops—big and small, urban and rural—are allowed to remain open 80 hours per week within the following framework:

- Legal business hours in Germany are now 8:00 A.M. to 8:00 P.M. Monday through Saturday.
- Late shopping is permitted on Thursdays (8:30 P.M.).
- On Sundays, only bakeries are permitted to open. Business hours are from 6:00 A.M. to 10:00 A.M.

In Switzerland, stores usually open at 8:00 A.M. during the business week. Business may be transacted on Saturdays until 5:00 P.M. or 6:00 P.M. On Sundays, all businesses are closed.

In Austria, stores are open around 8:00 A.M. Many, however, close for a two-hour lunch break. On Sundays, all businesses are closed.

Checkpoints

Use this section to test everything you've learned during this unit and review anything you're unsure of.

Can you ... ?

	Yes	No
● *say you've reserved a room*	❑	❑

Ich habe ein Zimmer bestellt.

	Yes	No
● *count from 101–999*	❑	❑

Hunderteins, hundertzwei... neunhundertneunundneunzig.

| ● *specify what kind of room you want* | ❑ | ❑ |

Ich möchte ein Einzelzimmer/Doppelzimmer mit Bad/Dusche.

| ● *ask whether breakfast is included* | ❑ | ❑ |

Ist Frühstück inklusive?

| ● *ask your way to various stores and services* | ❑ | ❑ |

Wo ist hier eine Post/ein Café/eine Buchhandlung?

| ● *say you don't understand* | ❑ | ❑ |

Ich verstehe nicht.

| ● *say "Pardon?"* | ❑ | ❑ |

Wie bitte?

| ● *ask someone to speak more slowly* | ❑ | ❑ |

Langsamer, bitte!

| ● *ask someone to repeat* | ❑ | ❑ |

Wie war das nochmal?

| ● *state the time* | ❑ | ❑ |

Es ist ein Uhr/halb drei/Viertel vor sieben.

Can you . . . ?   *Yes*   *No*

- *list the days of the week* . . . . ☐ . . . . . ☐
  Montag, Dienstag, Mittwoch, Donnerstag,
  Freitag, Samstag (Sonnabend), Sonntag

- *state opening times* . . . . ☐ . . . . . ☐
  Wir haben montags von acht Uhr bis siebzehn Uhr geöffnet.

Learning tips

*As you drive or cycle around, or take the dog for a walk, think
about the directions you are taking. Tell yourself where to go
(left, right, around the corner)—in German.*

Do you want to learn more?

*Collect German-language brochures for hotels and tourist
attractions. They often give written instructions as well as maps
showing how to get there. See how many of the instructions you
recognize.*

For more practice, see Extra! on page A9.

Unit 5 will introduce you to some language for shopping. By the end, you'll know how to:

- ask where you can get an item
- describe what you are looking for
- make a purchase

Einkaufs-bummel 5

die Apotheke (-n)	pharmacy	kaufen	to buy
die Briefmarke (-n)	(postage) stamp	können (ich kann, er kann)	to be able
der Computer (-)	computer	die Kopfschmerztablette (-n)	headache tablet
die Dachterrasse	roof terrace	die Kosmetika (pl)	cosmetics
die Damenmode (-n)	ladies' fashion	der Kugelschreiber (-)	ballpoint pen
die Damenwäsche	lingerie	die Lebensmittel (pl)	food, groceries
dort	there	nächste	next
dritte	third	das Obst	fruit
der Einkaufsbummel (-)	shopping spree	der Obsthändler (-)	fruit seller
das Elektrogerät (-e)	electrical appliance	die Parfümerie (-n)	perfumery
das Erdgeschoss	first floor (US); ground floor (UK)	der/die Passant/-in	passer-by (male/female)
erste	first	das Porzellan	porcelain, china
die Etage (-n)	floor, story	der Schreibwarenladen (-läden)	stationery store
der Etagenplan (-pläne)	floor plan, store plan (in department store, etc.)	die Spielwaren (pl)	toys
		die Sportartikel (pl)	sports goods
gegenüber von (+ dat.)	opposite	trinken	to drink
die Haushaltswaren (pl)	household items	vierte	fourth
die Herrenmode (-n)	men's fashion	die Zeitung (-en)	newspaper
die Herrenwäsche	men's underwear	zweite	second

Wo kann ich hier einen Film kaufen?

Finding out where you can buy an item

RECORDING

1. *Which of these items does the speaker want to buy?*

a.

b.

c. US NEWS

d.

e. ASPIRIN

f.

g. 200 50

h.

2. *How would you ask where to buy each of these items?*

a. *a newspaper*

b. *a ballpoint pen*

c. *headache tablets*

d. *fruit*

e. *stamps*

f. *bread*

3. *When prompted, ask where you can buy each of the items from Activity 2. Listen to the directions you are given, and complete the key to the map.*

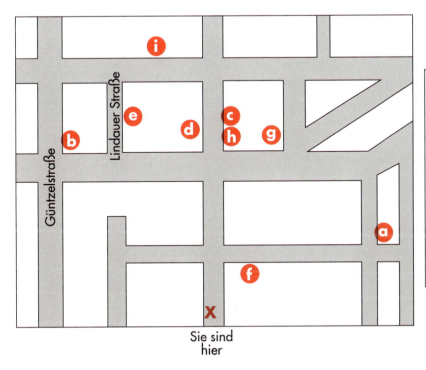

Schlüssel
a =
b =
c =
d =
e =
f =
g = Café
h = Bank
i = Supermarkt

Sie sind hier

Dort ist ein Obsthändler.   *There's a fruit seller.*

4. **Sie sind dran!** *Some people ask you the following questions. Give them directions in German to the appropriate places on the map.*

a. *Passant:* Entschuldigung! Wo kann ich hier einen Kaffee trinken?

   Sie: Gehen Sie _____.

b. *Passantin:* Entschuldigen Sie, wo kann ich hier Lebensmittel kaufen?

   Sie: _____.

5. *Check out the Close-up box first. Then listen to the recording and fill in the floor numbers.*

ETAGENPLAN

_____ Etage: Dachterrassen-Café

_____ Etage: Damenmode und Damenwäsche

_____ Etage: Elektrogeräte und Computer

_____ Etage: Haushaltswaren und Porzellan

_____ Etage: Herrenmode und Herrenwäsche

Erdgeschoss: Kosmetika und Parfümerie

_____ Etage: Spielwaren und Sportartikel

Close-up

Ordinal numbers 1–10

The basic pattern is to add **-te** to the cardinal number (one, two, etc.), but there are some irregular forms (underlined):

first.............. erste	sixth .... sechste
second .... zweite	seventh........... siebte
third .... dritte	eighth .... achte
fourth .... vierte	ninth............. neunte
fifth .... fünfte	tenth............. zehnte

When written as a figure, ordinals have a period after the number. So **(die) erste Etage** would be written **1. Etage**, and so on.

Word order

Remember: when there are two verbs in a sentence, the second verb often goes to the end:

Wo kann ich hier eine Zeitung kaufen?   Where can I buy a newspaper here?

Ich suche ein gestreiftes Hemd

Buying clothes, describing colors

Word Bank

aus+sehen	*to look like*
die Auswahl	*choice*
bestimmt	*definite; definitely*
blau	*blue*
die Bluse (-n)	*blouse*
einfach	*simple*
empfehlen	*to recommend*
etwas	*something*
die Farbe (-en)	*color*
für (+ acc.)	*for*
gemustert	*patterned*
gestreift	*striped*
die Größe (-n)	*size*
grün	*green*
das Hemd (-en)	*shirt*
die Hose (-n)	*pair of pants*
die Idee (-n)	*idea*
ihn	*him (accusative object)*
die Jacke (-n)	*jacket*
kennen	*to know (a person)*
das Leinenhemd (-en)	*linen shirt*
machen	*to make, to do*
modern	*modern*
na ja	*well… (expresses doubt)*
das Paar (-e)	*pair*
der Pullover (-)	*sweater*
der Rock (¨-e)	*skirt*
rot	*red*
schlank	*slim*
schlicht	*simple, plain*
schön	*beautiful*
die Seidenbluse (-n)	*silk blouse*
die Socke (-n)	*sock*
der Stil (-e)	*style*
suchen	*to look for*
viel	*much*
weiß	*white*
ziemlich	*quite*

1. *Look at this color wheel: rotate the names so that they fit the colors.*

rot

lila

orange

blau

gelb

grün

2. *Herr and Frau Kerschner have lost their daughter Sabine while shopping in a department store. Can you help the store detective to find Sabine?*

70 *German*

Wir haben ... verloren.	*We've lost ...*
Wie sieht sie aus?	*What does she look like?*
Warten Sie bitte.	*Please wait.*
Machen Sie sich keine Sorgen.	*Don't worry.*

RECORDING

3.

We have underlined the adjectives in the script. Can you see how the endings change?

Verkäufer: Kann ich Ihnen helfen?

Kundin: Ja, ich suche ein Hemd für meinen Mann.

Verkäufer: Wir haben eine große Auswahl ... Möchten Sie ein gestreiftes oder vielleicht ein gemustertes Hemd?

Kundin: Nein, lieber ein einfaches weißes Hemd.

Verkäufer: Da haben wir bestimmt etwas für Ihren Mann ... Ein schönes Leinenhemd. Was meinen Sie dazu?

Kundin: Oje! Das ist viel zu modern für ihn.

Verkäufer: Ja, dann ...

Kunde: Können Sie mir helfen? Ich suche eine Bluse für meine Frau.

Verkäuferin: Ja, natürlich. Suchen Sie einen bestimmten Stil oder eine bestimmte Farbe?

Kunde: Ähh, das weiß ich nicht. Können Sie mir etwas empfehlen?

Verkäuferin: Na ja, ich kenne Ihre Frau nicht. Vielleicht eine schlichte weiße Seidenbluse?

Kunde: Ja? ... Ja, das ist eine gute Idee.

Verkäuferin: Welche Größe hat Ihre Frau?

Kunde: Das weiß ich nicht... Sie ist ziemlich schlank.

Now fill in the correct adjective endings in the blanks:

Ich suche einen weiß_____ Pullover.

Ich suche eine weiß_____ Bluse.

Ich suche ein weiß_____ Hemd.

Können Sie mir etwas empfehlen?	*Can you recommend something (to me)?*
Was meinen Sie dazu?	*What do you think of that?*
Welche Größe hat Ihre Frau?	*What size does your wife have?*

4. **Sie sind dran!** *Say that you're looking for the following items.*

    a. A pair of blue pants or a blue skirt. (Specify what size.)

    b. A green blouse or a green shirt. (Specify what size.)

Womit kann ich dienen?	*How can I help you?*
Ich suche...	*I'm looking for...*
Ich habe Größe...	*I have size...*

Close up

Adjectives

If there is no article before the adjective and no noun after it, you just use the plain form of the adjective:

    Der Rock ist rot.   *The skirt is red.*

But if the adjective comes in front of the noun, it takes an ending. Here are the endings in the nominative case (when the noun is the subject and is preceded by an article):

masc.	der rote Rock	ein roter Rock
fem.	die rote Bluse	eine rote Bluse
neut.	das rote Hemd	ein rotes Hemd
plu.	die roten Hemden	

Ich nehme den großen Teddy

Specifying the item you want

1. *Which floors are these departments on?*

a. Toy department

b. Photography department

c. Perfumery

Wo finde ich so etwas?   **Where do I find something like that?**

W o r d   B a n k

das Auto (-s)	car	Prima!	Great!
die Fotoabteilung (-en)	photography department	die Puppe (-n)	doll
		rosarot	pink
der Fotoapparat (-e)	camera	der Schlips (-e)	tie
das Geschenk (-e)	gift	schrecklich	horrible
das Geschoss (-sse)	story, floor	das Schweinchen (-)	toy pig, little pig
hässlich	ugly	so etwas	something like that
Igitt!	Yuck!		
Klasse!	Great!	die Spielwarenabteilung (-en)	toy department
klein	small	der Stock (das Stockwerk)	story, floor
mittelgroß	medium-sized	der Teddy (-s)	teddy bear
nehmen (er nimmt)	to take	Toll!	Great!
niedlich	cute	Wunderschön!	Lovely!
das Parfüm	perfume		

More Colors	***Mehr Farben***				
beige	*beige*	grau	*gray*	schwarz	*black*
braun	*brown*	lila	*purple*	weiß	*white*

2.

Sie sind dran! *You're showing a German visitor around a department store. He wants to know where to find certain items. Answer his questions, using* **im... Stock, in der... Etage** *or* **im... Geschoss.** *Note: Floor one in Germany is the second floor (US) and the first floor (UK).*

Household Items and China	5
Photographic Equipment and Computers	4
Restaurant and Children's Clothes	3
Men's and Women's Fashions	2
Toys and Electrical Items	1
Cosmetics and Perfumery	G

Example: Wo ist die Fotoabteilung? Im vierten Stock.
   (Or: In der vierten Etage./Im vierten Geschoss.*)*

a. Wo sind die Haushaltswaren?

b. Wo kann ich einen Schlips kaufen?

c. Wo kann ich Parfüm für meine Frau kaufen?

d. Wo finde ich ein Geschenk für meinen kleinen Sohn?

3.

Which of these items are bought? Write down in German which items the speaker buys.

Example: Er nimmt den großen Teddy, ...

Sowas Niedliches!   *(They're) so cute!*

4. Which of these expressions are positive, and which are negative?
Wie finden Sie das?   What do you think of it?

Ausgezeichnet!

Hässlich!

Igitt!

Prima!

Klasse!

Schrecklich!

Toll!

Wunderschön!

Pronunciation

Now do the pronunciation exercise on the recording.

rot	rosa rot	das rosarote

Rhinozeros

Bier	hier

Close-up

The cases

As you already know, articles can change according to the use of a noun, There are two object cases in German, the accusative and the dative. As a general rule, the direct object takes the accusative and the indirect object takes the dative.

	Nominative *(subject)*		Accusative		Dative	
masc.	der	ein	den	einen	dem	einem
fem.	die	eine	die	eine	der	einer
neut.	das	ein	das	ein	dem	einem
plural	die		die		die	

Checkpoints

Use this section to test everything you've learned during this unit and review anything you're unsure of.

Can you... ?   Yes   No

- **ask where you can buy commonly needed items** .... ❏ ...... ❏
  Wo kann ich hier einen Film/einen Kugelschreiber/
  eine Zeitung/Brot/Obst kaufen?

- **give directions to a place** .... ❏ ...... ❏
  Gehen Sie geradeaus.
  Nehmen Sie die erste/zweite/dritte Straße links/rechts.

- **describe locations** .... ❏ ...... ❏
  Neben der Bank.
  Gegenüber von der Bank.
  In der Lindauer Straße.

- **give floor numbers** .... ❏ ...... ❏
  Erdgeschoss, erste/zweite/dritte/vierte/fünfte/sechste Etage

- **say what floor something is on** .... ❏ ...... ❏
  Es ist in der ersten Etage/im ersten Stock/im ersten Geschoss.

- **name common items of clothing** .... ❏ ...... ❏
  der Pullover, die Bluse, das Hemd, die Hose, der Rock

- **name colors** .... ❏ ...... ❏
  rot, blau, gelb, schwarz, weiß, grün, braun

- **say you're looking for an item of a specific color** .... ❏ ...... ❏
  Ich suche eine blaue Hose/einen blauen Rock.

- **say which item you want from a range** .... ❏ ...... ❏
  Ich nehme den großen Teddy, die blaue Hose.

- **say what you think of something** .... ❏ ...... ❏
  Toll! Prima! Wunderschön!
  Hässlich! Schrecklich! Igitt!

Learning tips

When you're learning the words for clothes and for colors, try to picture the article or the color in your mind as you're saying the name. When you get dressed in the morning, see if you can say to yourself the German names of the items you're putting on, and their colors.

Do you want to learn more?

*Look up the German names of items around your home or office in a dictionary. Then write out name tags in German and attach them to the items. (Remember to include **der/die/das**.) Self-adhesive notes are ideal for this, as they're easy to peel off.*

For more practice, see Extra! on page A11.

BAHNHOF

Unit 6 will introduce you to some language for travel. By the end, you'll know how to:

- buy a train ticket
- ask about times and connections
- rent a car
- ask how to get to a place by public transport

Unterwegs

6

Word Bank

ab *(+ dat.)*	*from*	das Gleis (-e)	*rail, platform*
ab+fahren	*depart*	hin und zurück	*round trip*
die Abfahrt (-en)	*departure*	die Klasse (-n)	*class*
an+kommen	*to arrive*	die Minute (-n)	*minute*
auf *(+ acc./dat.)*	*on*	müssen (ich muss, er muss)	*to have to*
die Bahn (-en)	*railroad, railway*	planmäßig	*scheduled*
bis	*until; by*	um+steigen	*to change (trains, etc.)*
einfach	*single; simple*		
einmal	*once*	der Zug (¨-e)	*train*
fahren (er fährt)	*to go (by vehicle)*	der Zuschlag (-schläge)	*supplement*
die Fahrkarte (-n)	*ticket (for travel)*	zweimal	*twice*

Mit der Bahn

Rail travel

1. *In what order do you hear these train announcements?*

a.

b.

c.

d.

planmäßige Abfahrt	*scheduled (time of) departure*
ICE/IC/EC (Intercity-Express/Intercity/EuroCity)	*categories of express trains, for which a supplement (Zuschlag) is payable*

2. *Which of the following tickets does each speaker ask for?*
(Some of the tickets are not asked for at all.)

a. *a one-way to Bremen*

b. *a round-trip to Bremen*

c. *two round-trips to Mannheim*

d. *a round-trip to Mannheim*

e. *two one-ways to Mannheim*

f. *two one-ways to Vienna*

g. *two round-trips to Vienna*

h. *a round-trip to Vienna*

3. Listen to the conversation, then complete the answers to the questions.

a. Um wie viel Uhr fährt der Zug? Der Zug fährt...

b. Wo muss man umsteigen? Man muss...

c. Was kostet die Fahrt insgesamt? Die Fahrt...

d. Was kostet der Zuschlag? Der Zuschlag...

e. Wo fährt der Zug ab? Der Zug fährt...

Wie komme ich am besten dorthin?   *What's the best way for me to get there?*

4. Look at this ticket, then fill in the blanks in the conversation.

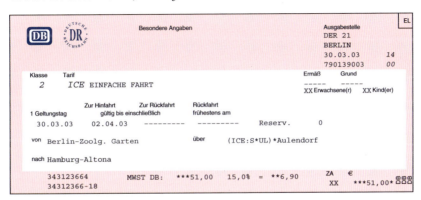

Beamter: Bitte schön?

    Sie: Einmal _____.

Beamter: Erste oder zweite Klasse?

    Sie: _____.

Beamter: Fahren Sie mit dem ICE oder mit dem EC?

    Sie: _____.

Beamter: Das macht dann einundfünfzig Euro
inklusive ICE-Zuschlag.

Did You Know?

Most towns and cities have an efficient and comprehensive public transportation system. The larger cities have buses, a **Straßenbahn** network, a **U-Bahn** network, <u>and</u> an **S-Bahn** network. For the **U-Bahn** and the **S-Bahn,** you have to buy your ticket before boarding the train; for buses you can buy tickets in advance or from the driver, and some streetcars have ticket vending machines on board, as well as at the stops.

Most types of tickets have to be stamped in a machine when you board the vehicle (or beforehand for the **U-Bahn** and **S-Bahn**). It's not enough to have bought a ticket, you must <u>stamp</u> it as well to have the right to travel. Plainclothes ticket inspectors make frequent checks, and anyone caught without a valid ticket can expect a hefty on-the-spot fine!

5. **Sie sind dran!** *Buy these tickets:*

a. *You are traveling from Hamburg to Berlin. You want a round-trip (return) ticket for two people, second class.*

b. *You are traveling from Cologne (**Köln**) to Frankfurt. You want a one-way ticket for one person, first class.*

Nichts zu danken.   *Think nothing of it. (Literally: Nothing to thank.)*

Close-up

fahren *and* gehen

In Unit 4 we met **gehen** "to go (on foot)." **Fahren** is always used when travel by vehicle is implied.

Adjective endings, nominative case

After **der/die** (singular)/**das**, adjectives <u>always</u> take the ending **-e**:

der letzte Bus   die letzte U-Bahn   das letzte Auto   *the last bus/subway/car*

After **die** (plural), adjectives <u>always</u> take the ending **-en**:

die letzten Busse

Ohne Kilometerbegrenzung

Renting a car

Word Bank

ab+biegen	to turn off	die Kreditkarte (-n)	credit card
ab+steigen	to get off, dismount	die Limousine (-n)	sedan car, saloon car
ähnlich	similar		
an+halten	to stop (in car)	mieten	to hire; rent
das Auto (-s)	car	mittlerer/e/es	medium-sized
die Begrenzung	limit, border	parken	to park
beide	both	die Parkgebühr (-en)	parking fee
brauchen	to need	die Parkuhr (-en)	parking meter
die Einbahnstraße (-n)	one-way street	die Preisklasse (-n)	price class
[r]ein+fahren	to turn in, enter	die Preisliste (-n)	price list
der Fahrzeugtyp (-en)	type of vehicle	das Problem (-e)	problem
der Führerschein (-e)	driver's license	Rad fahren	to cycle
die Geldbuße	fine	das Schild (-er)	sign
die Haftpflichtversicherung	liability insurance	die Versicherung (-en)	insurance
Halt!	Stop!	der Wagen (-)	car
heute	today	Was ist los?	What's the matter?
der Kleinwagen (-)	small car	Wie lange?	How long?
der Kombi (-s)	station wagon		

1. *What will the total price be for each of the customers?*

EUROMOBIL inkl. km

Fahrzeugtyp	Preisklasse	1–3 Tage in € pro Tag	4 u. mehr Tage in € pro Tag
Kleinwagen			
	A	79,–	70,–
	B	80,–	73,–
	C	85,–	75,–
	D	97,–	79,–
	E	110,–	97,–
Kombi-Wagen			
	C	85,–	75,–
	D	97,–	79,–
	E	110,–	97,–

inkl. 15% MwSt.
inkl. Haftpflichtversicherung

Das wäre Preisklasse B.
That would be price class B.

inkl. = inklusive
included, including

Ja, ist mir recht.
Yes, (that's) fine by me.

MwSt. = Mehrwertsteuer
sales tax, VAT

2. **Sie sind dran!** *Rent a medium-sized station wagon* **(einen mittleren Kombi)** *for seven days.*

3. *Listen to the four dialogues. Decide whether the policeman is expressing permission, obligation, and/or prohibition in each case.*

Was machen Sie da?
What are you doing (there)?

4. *Complete these sentences with* **darf** *or* **muss***, as most appropriate.*

 a. Hier _____ man rechts abbiegen.

 c. Hier _____ man nicht über 30 fahren.

 b. Hier _____ man anhalten.

 d. Hier _____ man nicht Rad fahren.

Close-up

(nicht) müssen *and* (nicht) dürfen

To say that someone <u>must</u> do something, use **müssen***. To say that someone <u>may</u> (i.e., is permitted to) do something, use* **dürfen***.*

Sie müssen anhalten.	You must stop.
Sie dürfen anhalten.	You may stop.

To say that someone must not do something, use **nicht dürfen***. Watch out:* **Sie müssen nicht** *means "you don't have to." It doesn't mean "you must not!"*

Sie dürfen nicht anhalten.	You must not stop.
Sie müssen nicht anhalten (aber Sie dürfen).	You don't have to stop (but you may).

Modalverbs

Verbs that are used with another verb to modify its meaning are called modalverbs. For example, **müssen** *"to have to,"* **dürfen** *"to be permitted to," and* **können** *"to be able to" are usually used as modalverbs. When a modalverb is used, the other verb goes to the end of the sentence. The infinitive form of that verb is used. Compare these two sentences:*

Ich <u>parke</u> in der Uhlandstraße.	I <u>park</u> in Uhlandstraße.
Ich <u>muss/darf/kann</u> in der Uhlandstraße <u>parken</u>.	I <u>must/may/can park</u> in Uhlandstraße.

German literally says: "I <u>must</u> in the Uhlandstraße <u>park</u>."

Separable verbs *(cont'd.)*

*There are many separable verbs relating to travel and transport (***ankommen, absteigen,** *etc.). If you use an auxiliary verb with a separable verb, remember to use the infinitive form of the separable verb, and put it at the end of the sentence:*

Ich <u>biege</u> rechts <u>ein</u>.	I turn to the right.
Ich <u>muss</u> rechts <u>einbiegen</u>.	I must turn to the right.

In der Großstadt

Making your way around town by public transport

Word Bank

abends	*in the evening(s)*	die Linie (-n)	*line*
alle... Minuten	*every... minutes*	oft	*often*
aus+steigen	*to get out*	der Platz (¨-e)	*square*
der Bahnhof (-höfe)	*(rail) station*	die Richtung (-en)	*direction*
die Brücke (-n)	*bridge*	die S-Bahn (= Schnellbahn)	*urban light railway*
der Bus (-se)	*bus*	die Straßenbahn	*trolley bus; streetcar*
dauern	*to last*	die U-Bahn (= Untergrundbahn)	*subway*
ein+werfen	*insert*	um+steigen	*to change (trains, etc.)*
der Fahrschein (-e)	*ticket (for bus, etc.)*	die Viertelstunde (-n)	*quarter of an hour*
das Geld	*money*	wählen	*to select*
die Großstadt (-städte)	*metropolitan area*	das Wechselgeld	*change (money)*
halber/e/es	*half (a)*	weit	*far*
im = in dem	*in the (masculine or neuter)*	der Zoo (-s)	*zoo*
die Insel (-n)	*island*	zu Fuß	*on foot*
jeder/e/es	*every, each*	zur = zu der	*to the (feminine)*
letzter/e/es	*last*		

1. *Listen to the recording. How many stops will the tourist have to travel to reach these places from Yorckstraße Station?*

a. die Museumsinsel (*Museum Island*)

b. der Zoo

c. das Nikolaiviertel (*the Nikolai Quarter*)

d. der Kurfürstendamm *or* „der Ku'damm"

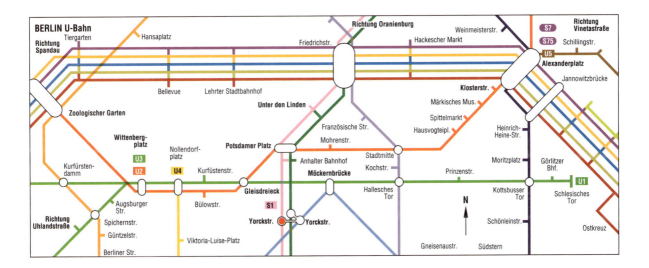

Von dort können Sie zu Fuß gehen.
From there you can walk (go on foot).

Das dauert eine Viertelstunde.
It takes a quarter of an hour.

Richtung Vinetastraße
(in the) direction (of) Vinetastraße

2. **Sie sind dran!** *You're at Alexanderplatz. You're asked how to get to the following places:*

a. Bahnhof Zoo (Zoologischer Garten)

b. Wittenbergplatz

c. Unter den Linden

3. *Match each of these bus timetables with the appropriate dialogue(s).*

A.	06 Uhr	00	20	40			
	07 Uhr	00	20	40			
B.	14 Uhr	05	15	25	35	45	55
	15 Uhr	05	15	25	35	45	55
C.	22 Uhr	12	27	42	57		
	23 Uhr	12	27	42			
D.	06 Uhr	45					
	07 Uhr	15	45				

Now look at the timetables again and say in German how often each bus runs.

4. *On official notices, instructions are often expressed with infinitives. Match these illustrations of public transportation to the instructions below.*

a.

b.

c.

d. Fahrausweise

SWR ● SWR ● SWR
08.01.03 € 1,20
041
3730

Wechselgeld und Fahrschein nehmen.

Fahrschein im Bus entwerten.

Geld einwerfen.

Fahrschein wählen.

Pronunciation

Do the pronunciation exercise on the recording. Then practice pronouncing these words:

ich	mich	spreche
ach	nach	Sprache

Close-up

Adjective endings

As you know, adjectives take an ending when they come in front of the noun. The endings differ, depending on which article is used. You've already seen the endings with the <u>indefinite</u> article. The endings with the <u>definite</u> article are simpler—adjectives <u>always</u> end in **-e** or **-en**:

Accusative

den blau<u>en</u> Rock ....the blue skirt

die blau<u>e</u> Bluse............the blue blouse

das blau<u>e</u> Hemd............the blue shirt

die blau<u>en</u> Hemden.......the blue shirts

Dative

im erst<u>en</u> Stock....................on the first floor

in der erst<u>en</u> Etage...............on the first floor

im erst<u>en</u> Geschoss ....on the first floor

in den erst<u>en</u> Etagen ....on the first floors

Contracted forms

Notice that **in dem** is usually written and pronounced **im**. Other contracted forms that you'll meet: **zu + dem = zum, zu + der = zur**.

Word order (cont'd.)

In Unit 4 you saw that word order can be changed for emphasis, as long as the verb comes second in the sentence. It's important to realize though that the verb doesn't have to be the second <u>word</u> in the sentence, it has to be the second <u>expression</u>. For example, a noun with its article and an adjective describing the noun counts as one expression. So in the sentence:

Der letzte Bus <u>fährt</u> um elf.   The last bus goes at eleven.

—the phrase **der letzte Bus** is the first expression, and **fährt** is the second expression. Look at these sentences:

Von dort <u>können</u> Sie zu Fuß gehen.   From there you can walk (go on foot).

Sie <u>können</u> von dort zu Fuß gehen.   You can walk from there.

Von dort is one expression, so **können** is the second expression in both of these sentences.

Checkpoints

Use this section to test everything you've learned during this unit and review anything you're unsure of.

Can you... ?

Yes   No

- *ask for a single ticket for one person to Bremen* .... ☐ ...... ☐
  Einmal Bremen einfach, bitte.

- *ask for a round-trip (return) ticket for two to Hanover* .... ☐ ...... ☐
  Zweimal Hannover hin und zurück, bitte.

- *say you would like to rent a car for seven days* .... ☐ ...... ☐
  Ich möchte ein Auto für sieben Tage (mieten).

- *say that someone may/must do something* .... ☐ ...... ☐
  Sie dürfen/müssen hier parken.

- *say that someone mustn't/need not do something* .... ☐ ...... ☐
  Sie dürfen/müssen hier nicht parken.

- *give directions how to get to a place by public transportation* .... ☐ ...... ☐
  Fahren Sie mit der S1 bis Potsdamer Platz.
  Steigen Sie in die U2 (Richtung Vinetastraße) um.

- *ask how often a service runs* .... ☐ ...... ☐
  Wie oft fahren die Busse/fährt die U-Bahn?

- *say how often a service runs* .... ☐ ...... ☐
  Die Busse fahren alle zwanzig Minuten/jede halbe Stunde.
  Die U-Bahn fährt alle zehn Minuten/jede Viertelstunde.

Learning tips

*When listening to recordings in German, do your best to imitate
the exact rhythm and intonation of the speakers. If you can
reproduce the rhythm and intonation accurately, other
pronunciation errors, such as mispronouncing certain sounds, will
not be as noticeable and your German will be easier to understand.*

Do you want to learn more?

*Get a hold of some street, subway, and bus maps for cities in
German-speaking countries. Study the names of the major sights
you'd like to visit, the streets on which they are located, and the
major subway stations. Practice using the language you'd need
to travel on public transportation to and from different places.*

For more practice, see Extra! on page A13.

1 Extra!

RECORDING

1. *Listen to the flight announcements. Write down the flight numbers, then match each one to the photo of the appropriate destination.*

a.　b.　c.

d.　e.　f.

RECORDING

2. *Listen again and complete the information on the departures board.*

✈ ABFLUG					
Flugnummer	**nach/über**	**Abflug** **planmäßig**	**erwartet**	**Flugsteig**	**Kommentar**
AA 1230	New York	1540	1540	_____	Einstieg
BA 456	_____	1550	1550	_____	Einstieg
QA _____	Sydney	1605	1605		Abfert.
_____ 7245	Moskau	1615	1615	15	Abfert.
AF 1170	_____	1625	1655	_____	verspätet
LH _____	_____	1630	1630	12	Abfert.

3. *Listen to the interviews, then answer the questions below.*

   a. Wohnt Frau Tränker in Berlin?

   b. Kommt sie aus Berlin? Woher kommt sie?

   c. Woher kommt Herr Schumann?

   d. Wo wohnt er?

4. *Here are some of the questions and answers from Activity 3. Can you match the questions to the answers?*

   1. Wie ist Ihr Name?

   2. Sind Sie von hier?

   3. Woher sind Sie?

   a. Nein, ich bin nicht von hier.

   b. Ich bin aus Frankfurt.

   c. Ich heiße Thomas Renck.

5. *How well do you know the German-speaking lands? The towns on the map on the following page have their vowels missing—can you complete their names?*

I. K l	8. D r t m n d	15. S r b r c k n	22. B r n
2. R s t c k	9. K l n	16. H d l b r g	23. G n f
3. S c h w r n	10. B n n	17. N r n b r g	24. n n s b r c k
4. H m b r g	II. r f r t	18. S t t t g r t	25. S l z b r g
5. B r m n	12. L p z g	19. M n c h n	26. L n z
6. H n n v r	13. D r s d n	20. B s l	27. W n
7. B r l n	14. F r n k f r t	21. Z r c h	28. G r z

2 Extra!

Spitze
am Hauptbahnhof
günstige Preise, hohe Qualität

Bratwurst
8er
Packung = 500g
4,99

Vollkornbrot
aus unserer Bäckerei
–,79

Orangen
1kg.
1,79

ofenfrisches
Brot
aus unserer
Bäckerei

Orangensaft
1 Liter
1,89

Getränke—
einmalig billig!

Brandenburger
Pilsener
0,5 Liter Dose
–,89

Sekt weiß
0,75 Liter
Flasche
3,49

Milch
1 Liter
–,59

Fruchtsaft
Apfelsaft
Grapefruitsaft
Alle
1,40

Spargel
aus Spanien
oder Griechenland
weiß/violett
Klasse 1
500g Bund
1,99

Käse
100g
1,20

Schokolade
aus der Schweiz
1,69

Oliven
aus Spanien (schwarz oder grün)
400g Dose
2,50

---

1. Study the ad for Spitze supermarkets. Then answer the questions

   a. Wie viel kostet eine Dose Bier?

   b. Wie viel kosten die Orangen?

   c. Was kostet 1,89 Euro?

   d. Wie viel kostet die Milch?

   e. Wie viel kosten die Oliven?

   f. Was kostet –,79 Euro?

2. *Can you complete these sentences with words from the box?*

   a. Ich möchte eine _____ Sekt.

   b. Ich möchte _____ Kaffee, bitte.

   c. Ein _____ Trauben, bitte.

   d. Was kosten zwei _____ Bier?

   e. Ich möchte _____ Cola, bitte.

   f. Ich möchte _____ Brot.

einen	eine	Flasche
Kilo	Dosen	ein

RECORDING

3. **Sie sind dran!** *Here's part of a menu from Café Kranzler. Order a pastry and a drink of your choice from the menu.*

✥§ *Menu* ੬✥

Sachertorte	€ 2,80
Bienenstich	€ 1,90
Streuselkuchen	€ 2,90
Spezialität des Hauses	
Kanzlerschnitte	€ 3,00
(Schoko-Sahneschnitte mit Ananasgeschmack)	
Tasse Schokolade	€ 2,50
Tasse Kaffee	€ 2,20
Glas Tee	€ 1,90

RECORDING

1. Listen to Harry Arnold introducing the contestants on **Goldene Stunde**, then answer the questions below.

| Jörg | Jutta | Christa | Uwe | Manuela |

a. Is the Teske family from Schwerin or Magdeburg?

b. Can you label the contestants from left to right? (The names are in the box.)

c. Who is married to Jörg?

d. What is Uwe's relationship to Manuela?

e. How is Jutta related to Manuela?

f. What is Christa's relationship to Uwe?

g. What is Manuela's relationship to Jörg?

2. *Jane Owen has started writing to a German pen pal, Inge Naumann. Here's Inge's first letter back. Can you fill in the blanks with the words from the box?*

Potsdam, den 12. August

Liebe Jane,
vielen _____ für den netten Brief. Ich möchte jetzt etwas von mir und meiner _____ erzählen.
Ich bin _____ Jahre alt und mit Jochen _____. Wir wohnen seit drei Jahren hier in _____, aber wir kommen beide aus Rostock.
Wir haben eine _____ : Sie heißt Maria und ist _____ Jahre alt.
Ich bin _____ , und Jochen ist _____ .
Wir _____ beide _____ - aber nicht sehr gut! Wir machen oft _____ in Irland und möchten gern mal in die _____ reisen.
Hier sind zwei _____ . Im ersten sehen Sie Jochen (links), seine Schwester und seinen Bruder. Im zweiten sehen Sie mich und Maria mit Stefan - Marias Cousin.

Liebe Grüße,

Ihre Inge Naumann

Dank	Heilpraktiker	Tierärztin	verheiratet
Englisch	Potsdam	Tochter	zweiunddreißig
Familie	sieben	Urlaub	USA
Fotos	sprechen		

Tierarzt/-ärztin   *vet*

Heilpraktiker/-in   *non-medical practitioner*

3. *One of these illustrations doesn't belong with the letter on the previous page. Which one is it?*

4. **Sie sind dran!** *Now write a similar letter about yourself and your family. Begin your letter with* **Liebe**... *if you're writing to a woman, and with* **Lieber**... *if you're writing to a man. If you're writing to both, write* **Liebe..., lieber...** *You can finish with* **Liebe Grüße** *(informal) or* **Mit freundlichen Grüßen** *(slightly more formal). You write* **Ihr** *if you're a man and* **Ihre** *if you're a woman, and then sign your name.*

4 *Extra*!

RECORDING

1.

Listen to the conversation at Potsdam Tourist Information.

Which of the following events are offered by the tourist information?

a. ein Ballett

b. zwei Konzerte in der Philharmonie

c. ein Konzert in Potsdam

RECORDING

2.

Rabea's keeping a note of what she's doing and when. Match the events with the days Rabea plans to participate in them.

a. Mittwoch, 12.45 Uhr

b. Dienstag, 12 Uhr

c. Montag, 11 Uhr

d. Sonntag, 10 Uhr

e. Samstag, 20 Uhr

A. ein Konzert in der Philharmonie

B. eine Havelrundfahrt

C. eine Führung durch das Neue Palais

D. ein Besuch der Filmstudios

E. eine Stadtrundfahrt durch Potsdam

3. *Listen to the audio tour of the Tiergarten park in Berlin. Can you put names to the sights? One of the sights doesn't belong on the map. Which one is it?*

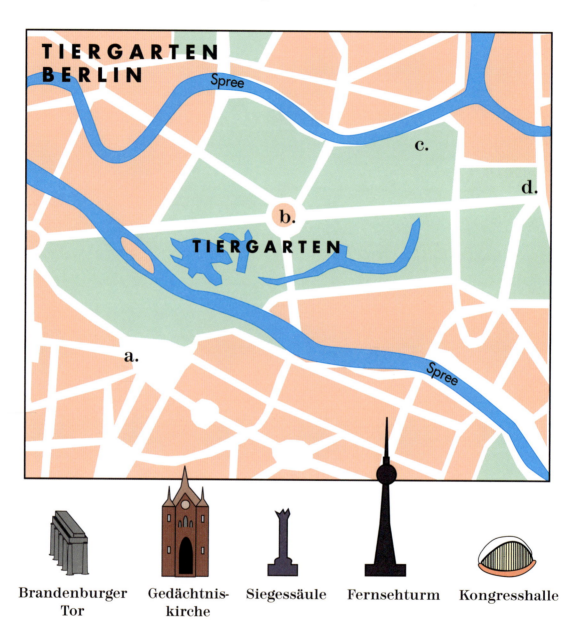

Brandenburger Tor   Gedächtnis-kirche   Siegessäule   Fernsehturm   Kongresshalle

5 Extra!

RECORDING

1. Ein junger Mann möchte gern _____.

   a. eine schöne Party

   b. eine große Torte

   c. einen Videorecorder

RECORDING

2. Anke und Rabea wünschen sich zum Geburtstag _____.

   a. viel Schokolade und Bücher

   b. ganz viel Geld und einen Schrank voll CDs

   c. eine große Pflanze für ihr Auto

3. **Sie sind dran!** *Now write down your wish list for a holiday or your birthday. Use* **Ich wünsche mir...** *and the thing you want–in the accusative case. If you don't know all the words you need, consult your dictionary.*

_____

_____

_____

_____

4. *These two people accidentally swapped shopping bags when they left the department store café. Now they're phoning the store to list the things they've lost. Can you complete their descriptions? All the words you need are in the box.*

Er: Ich habe ein _____ Hemd und eine _____

und _____ Unterhose und ein Paar grüne Socken

verloren.

Sie: Ich habe einen _____ Rock, eine _____

Bluse, einen _____ BH und eine _____ und

_____ Strumpfhose verloren.

orange	grünen	rosarote	grüne
gelben	rote	weiße	blaues

Ich habe... verloren.   *I have lost...*

6 Extra!

Traffic vocabulary

abgeben	*to drop off/leave*
der Arbeitsort	*place of work*
die Autobahn (-en)	*freeway, motorway, highway*
Autofahrer/-in (-/-nen)	*car driver*
deshalb	*that is why*
eigen	*one's own*
entfernt	*(distance) away*
die Fahrbahn (-en)	*carriageway, lane*
das Fahrzeug (-e)	*means of transportation*
es geht gut/schlecht	*it goes well/badly*
das Glatteis	*black ice*
die Hauptverkehrszeit	*peak hours (for traffic)*
die Mitfahrerzentrale (-n)	*ride sharing agency*
der Mittelklassewagen (-)	*midsize sedan*
der Nebel	*fog*
der PKW (**P**ersonen**k**raft**w**agen) (-)	*passenger car*
in der Regel	*usually, normally*
restlich	*the rest of*
die Schubkarre (-n)	*pushcart*
stadteinwärts	*to town*
der Stadtrand	*city limits*
der Stau (-s)	*traffic jam*
stockender Verkehr	*slow traffic*
die Stockung (-en)	*hold-up, delay*
die Straßenbahn (-en)	*trolley, streetcar*
südlich	*southern*
der Unfall (-fälle)	*accident*
unterwegs	*on the road*
der Verkehr	*traffic*
das Verkehrsmittel (-)	*means of transport*
der Verlag	*publishing house*
die Verspätung (-en)	*delay*
Was hätten Sie sich denn vorgestellt?	*What did you have in mind?*
weit	*far*

1. *Listen to the interviews, then decide which of the following statements are <u>correct</u>.*

a. Alle Leute fahren mit dem Auto zur Arbeit.

b. Keiner fährt mit dem Zug zur Arbeit.

c. Im Sommer fahren viele mit der Straßenbahn ins Büro.

d. Zwei Frauen bringen ihre Kinder zur Schule.

e. Eine Frau nimmt ihre Kinder mit, weil sie Lehrerin ist.

f. Alle Frauen fahren alleine zur Arbeit.

2. *Listen to the traffic report, then circle on the map where the problems are and list them in the order you hear them. Use the vocabulary on page A13 to help you along.*

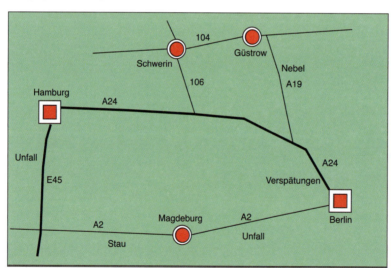

Norden	*North*
(nördlich)	*north (of)*
Osten	*East*
(östlich)	*east (of)*
Süden	*South*
(südlich)	*South (of)*
Westen	*West*
(westlich)	*west (of)*

3. *You're staying at a hotel. Frieda has faxed you a map, showing how to get to her party. You're phoning Frieda to ask the way. Listen to Frieda's description of how to get to the party. Follow the instructions. On what street does she live?*

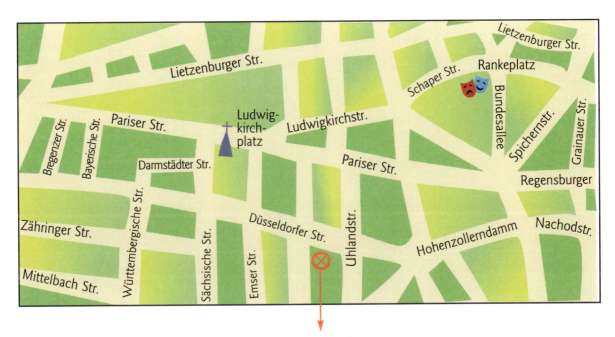

your hotel

Test 1:

Review of Units 1–3

1. *Can you complete the word grid? All the clues are related to food, drink, and shopping. Write the answers in capital letters.*

1. *Spicy sausage dish.* (10)

2. Sechs *(pieces)* bitte. (5)

3. Ich möchte ein _____ Kaffee. (8)

4. Darf ich _____? Mmm, es schmeckt gut! (9)

5. *Alcoholic drink.* (4)

6. _____ nehme vierhundert Gramm von dem Emmentaler. (3)

7. Eine Brat _____ mit Brot bitte. (5)

8. *A dairy product.* (5)

9. _____ Sie Orangen?—Ja, natürlich! (5)

10. Was darf es _____? (4)

11. Sonst noch _____? (5)

2. *Can you complete these sums?*

a. Achtzehn plus neunzehn ist _____.

b. Einundneunzig minus neunundzwanzig ist _____.

c. Achtundvierzig plus _____ ist siebenundachtzig.

d. Hundert minus fünfundvierzig ist _____.

e. Dreizehn plus _____ minus vierundzwanzig ist zwölf.

3. *Complete the sentence with the correct forms of the verbs in parentheses.*

a. Das _____ (sein) Sabine. Sie _____ (kommen) aus Köln. Sie _____ (sprechen) Deutsch, Englisch und Französisch. Sie _____ (sein) verheiratet und _____ (haben) eine Tochter. Ihre Tochter _____ (heißen) Jutta.

b. Ich _____ (heißen) Klaus. Ich _____ (kommen) aus Bremen. Ich _____ (sprechen) Englisch und etwas Holländisch—und Deutsch, natürlich! Ich _____ (sein) geschieden und _____ (haben) zwei Kinder.

c. Ich _____ (sein) Manfred und das _____ (sein) meine Frau Inge. Wir _____ (kommen) beide aus München. Wir _____ (haben) drei Söhne. Sie _____ (heißen) Ralf, Jürgen, und Clemens.

4. *Look at the family tree, then complete the sentences by providing the correct words for the family relationships in the blanks.*

Example: Christas <u>Mann</u> heißt Werner.

1. Christa _____ heißt Dagmar und ihre _____ heißen Matthias und Thomas.

2. Matthias hat zwei _____: eine _____ und einen _____.

3. Dagmar ist verheiratet: Ihr _____ heißt Erich.

4. Dagmar und Erich haben zwei _____: Olivia und Mark.

5. Dagmar ist Marks _____ und Erich ist sein _____.

6. Christa ist Olivias _____ und Werner ist Olivias _____.

7. Erichs _____ heißt Dagmar.

8. Werners _____ heißen Olivia und Mark.

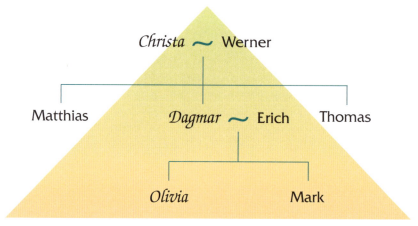

5. *Can you write sentences following the same pattern as the example?*

Example: Jonathan kommt aus England. Er ist Engländer. Er spricht Englisch.

a. Sylvia kommt aus England. . . .

b. Bob kommt aus den USA. . . .

c. Jasmin kommt aus der Türkei. . . .

d. Hans kommt aus Deutschland. . . .

e. Isabelle kommt aus Frankreich. . . .

f. Marco kommt aus Italien. . . .

g. Will kommt aus Australien. . . .

h. Mikhail kommt aus Russland. . . .

i. Delphine kommt aus der Schweiz. . . . (Französisch)

j. Erika kommt aus Österreich. . . .

6.

Write sentences stating what jobs these people do, following the pattern of the example:

Example: Gabi Franke: photographer
Gabi Franke ist Fotografin.

a. *Dieter Hanschke: construction worker*

b. *Jürgen Schumacher: hair stylist*

c. *Birgit Harms: teacher*

d. *Uwe Balzer: nurse*

e. *Renate Bachmann: cashier*

7.

In the word square there are 10 expressions for greeting someone or saying good-bye. How many of them can you find? They all run in a straight line—vertically, horizontally, or diagonally. We've done the first one for you.

_____

_____

_____

_____

_____

_____

_____

_____

_____

A	U	F	E	D	R	S	E	H	E	H	O	Ü	H
U	U	Ü	R	**G**	**U**	**T**	**E**	**N**	**T**	**A**	**G**	G	I
F	Ö	F	G	A	T	Ö	R	E	H	L	T	H	T
R	G	A	W	U	T	S	T	L	N	L	S	A	T
E	D	U	J	I	T	E	C	S	S	O	E	K	C
U	D	U	T	M	E	E	A	H	C	H	R	C	H
T	W	A	T	E	T	D	N	A	Ü	E	V	I	Ü
M	T	I	S	E	N	G	E	A	U	S	U	A	N
I	A	S	E	I	N	M	N	R	C	A	S	O	H
C	D	T	C	Y	S	M	O	S	H	H	B	Ü	H
H	D	H	F	W	E	T	O	R	R	Ö	T	S	T
F	T	E	N	A	B	E	D	R	G	Ö	R	H	G
A	U	F	W	I	E	D	E	R	S	E	H	E	N
U	F	W	I	E	D	E	H	Ü	S	S	N	E	N

Test 2:

Review of Units 4–6

1. *Can you complete the word grid? All the clues are related to travel and transportation. Write the answers in capital letters (use **ss** instead of **ß**.)*

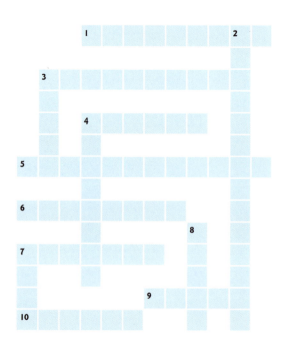

ACROSS

1.   *To change (trains etc.)* (9)

3.   *Ticket* (10)

4.   Hin und _____ (6)

5.   *Insurance* (12)

6.   *Direction* (8)

7.   *Departure* (7)

9.   Der Zug nach Mannheim fährt auf _____ 3 ab. (5)

10. *Once* (6)

DOWN

2.   Hier dürfen Sie nur in eine Richtung fahren. (14)

3.   Ich _____ nach Köln. (5)

4.   *Supplement* (8)

7.   Die Busse fahren _____ zehn Minuten. (4)

8.   *To go (on foot)* (5)

2. *How would you ask for these items in a store? Start each sentence with **Ich suche**...*

    Example: <u>Ich suche eine blaue Hose.</u>

    a.   *red skirt*

    b.   *green pants*

    c.   *black jacket*

    d.   *white shirt*

    e.   *blue pullover*

3.

Can you assign each of the items to the correct department of the store?

Parfüm

Rock

Puppe

Bluse

Brot

Herrenhose

Teddy

Schlips

COMPUTER

Kugelschreiber

Fleisch

ETAGENPLAN	
Dachterrasse:	*Café*
2. Etage:	*Elektrogeräte*
	Spielwaren
	Schreibwaren
1. Etage:	*Sportartikel*
	Herrenmode
Erdgeschoss:	*Damenmode*
	Kosmetika
	Lebensmittel

4.

This dialogue has been scrambled. Can you put the words in the correct order?

Hotel receptionist: . Guten Tag ? etwas für ich Kann Sie tun

Guest: . Ja . Doppelzimmer Dusche ein mit möchten Wir

Hotel receptionist: ? bleiben lange möchten Sie Wie

Guest: . bleiben drei möchten Nächte Wir

Hotel receptionist: , . Doppelzimmer ein frei haben Ja wir . Das kostet Euro Nacht pro einhundertzehn

Guest: ? Frühstück inbegriffen Ist

Hotel receptionist: , . Frühstück inbegriffen ist Ja

Guest: . es nehmen Wir

Hotel receptionist: . aus bitte das Formular Füllen Sie

5. *Answer each of the questions with full sentences, using the time shown on the clockface. Where times are shown in the 24-hour clock, answer using the 24-hour clock also.*

Examples: Wie spät ist es? <u>Es ist halb sieben.</u>

Wann fährt der Zug? Der Zug fährt <u>um achtzehn Uhr dreißig.</u>

a. Wie spät ist es?

b. Wann öffnet die Bibliothek?

c. Um wie viel Uhr fährt der Zug nach Freiburg?

d. Wann kommen Sie in München an?

e. Um wie viel Uhr kommen die Nachrichten?

a. 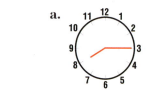   b.

c.    d. 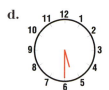   e.

6. *Can you write sentences following the same pattern as the example?*

Example: Rechts abbiegen. <u>Biegen Sie rechts ab.</u>

a. In Mannheim umsteigen.

b. Geradeaus fahren, dann links einbiegen.

c. Das Geld einwerfen.

d. Den Fahrschein im Bus entwerten.

e. Um elf Uhr abfahren.

7. *There are eight compound nouns in this string of letters. Each word overlaps with its neighbor by one letter. Can you find the nouns?*

R E N N F A H R E R U H E T A G E L D A U T O M A T A X I S T A N D A M E N
M O D E R D G E S C H O S S C H R E I B W A R E N L A D E N E U S E E L A N D

Answer Key

Unit 1

Pages 2–3

1. 1. *greeting, uncertain;* 2. *greeting, morning;* 3. *farewell, uncertain;* 4. *greeting, evening;* 5. *farewell, uncertain;* 6. *farewell, night*

2. 1. g + d; 2. a + c; 3. e + f

3. Guten Tag. /heiße (*your name*)./ Familienname (*last name*)./ Vorname, (*first name*).

4. geht es Ihnen; gut, danke; Ihnen

Pages 5–7

1. Petra; Klaus; Sabine; Sylvia; Käthe; Werner

2. 1. Steuer; 2. Gross; 3. Schmäh; 4. Schmitt

3. b and c

4. Guten Tag. Sind Sie Herr Schulz? Ich heiße/Ich bin/Mein Name ist (*your name*). (*Spell your name.*) (*Give your phone number.*) Auf Wiederhören.

5. A–Z 314 8919; Marion 894 7282; Rudi 782 0407; Gudrun Pfaff 815 7482 (*correct*)

6. a. Guten Tag. Mein Name ist Henneberg— Horst Henneberg.
   b. Guten Abend, Herr Schmidt! Wie geht es Ihnen?
   c. Guten Morgen. Ich bin Fritz Knoll.
   d. Kommen Sie herein.

Pages 10–13

1. Harald Schwarz, Wien; Sara Müller, München; Petra Hansen, Kiel; Peter Krüger, Berlin; Gabriele Römer, Zürich

2. *Your answers should go something like this:* Guten Tag, ich bin Mary Jones. Ich komme aus Washington.

3. Susan Bell: *New York*; Dieter Pohl: *Vienna*; Herr Nowakowski: *Poland*; Otto Hinze: *Berne (Switzerland)*

4. Guten Tag. Ich bin... (*Variation possible here, e.g. you could say: Ich heiße...*) Ich bin aus... Woher sind Sie?

5. 1. Zwei plus vier ist sechs. 2 + 4 = 6
   2. Fünf minus zwei ist drei. 5 – 2 = 3
   3. Sieben plus fünf ist zwölf. 7 + 5 = 12
   4. Achtzehn minus acht ist zehn. 18 – 8 = 10
   5. Zwanzig minus sieben ist dreizehn. 20 – 7 = 13
   6. Siebzehn minus acht ist neun. 17 – 8 = 9

6. ich komme; wir kommen; Sie kommen; er/sie/es kommt; sie kommen

Unit 2

Pages 18–20

1. Bitte; möchte; Bratwurst; Sonst; eine Cola; danke

2. Bratwurst mit Brot; Currywurst; Pommes (frites)

3. 1. 1,20; 2. 3,50; 3. 18; 4. 80; 5. 30; 6. 13,10; 7. 40,50; 8. 17; 9. 7,70; 10. 9,90

4. 1. Ich möchte eine Currywurst; 2. Ich möchte ein kleines Bier; 3. Ich möchte ein Käsebrot; 4. Ich möchte eine Cola

Pages 21–23

1. a. D; b. B; c. A; d. C

2. 1. *Tea: Ceylon, with lemon;* 2. *Filter coffee;* 3. *Beer: Pilsener, 0.4 l;* 4. *Orange juice*

3. a. (Ich möchte) einen Tee (bitte). b. (Ich möchte) einen Kaffee (bitte). c. (Ich möchte) ein Bier (bitte). d. (Ich möchte) einen Orangensaft (bitte).

4. 1. b; 2. a; 3. c

Pages 25–28

1. 1. e; 2. c; 3. b; 4. d; 5. a
2. 1. Guten Tag. Haben Sie Edamer Käse?; Ich nehme vierhundert Gramm.; Nein, danke.
   2. Haben Sie schwarze Oliven?; Darf ich probieren?; Ich nehme hundert Gramm.; Nein, danke.
   3. (Ich möchte/Ich hätte gern) fünf Orangen, bitte.; Ja, fünf Nektarinen.; Nein, danke.
3. fünfundzwanzig, sechsundzwanzig, siebenundzwanzig, achtundzwanzig, neunundzwanzig, dreißig, einunddreißig, zweiunddreißig, dreiunddreißig, vierunddreißig, fünfunddreißig, sechsunddreißig, siebenunddreißig, achtunddreißig, neununddreißig, vierzig
4. a. 34; b. 30; c. 79; d. 35; e. 28; f. 62; g. 93; h. 18; i. 41; j. 65

Unit 3

Pages 34–36

1. c. *Yes, I'm married.*
   b. *No, I'm still single.*
   e. *No, I'm divorced.*
   d. *No, but I have a partner.*
   a. *Yes, but we're separated.*
2. 1. *one daughter;* 2. *one son;* 3. *two sons;* 4. *no children;* 5. *one son and two daughters;* 6. *no children*
3. a. Mutter; b. Vater; c. Bruder; d. Mann; e. Schwester; f. Schwester; g. Sohn; h. Tochter
4. a. Nein, ihre Eltern heißen Hedwig und Clemens.
   b. Nein, ihre Schwestern heißen Birgit und Steffi.
   c. Ihre Tochter heißt Julia.
   d. Ja, ihr Mann heißt Klaus.
   e. Nein, ihr Sohn heißt Raphael.
5. a. Sind Sie verheiratet?
   b. Wie heißt Ihre Frau?
   c. Haben Sie Geschwister?
   d. Haben Sie Kinder?

Pages 39–42

1. 1. Katharina Müller ist Architektin. *(architect)*
   2. Jochen Weiß ist Fotograf. *(photographer)*
   3. Klaus-Dieter Stolz ist Kundenberater. *(customer adviser)*
   4. Paula Prescher ist Ärztin. *(doctor)*
   5. Stefan Dombrowski ist Computertechniker. *(technician)*
2. a. Dieter Speck ist Taxifahrer. Er ist nicht… *(Free answers:* Künstler)
   b. Sonja Brückner ist Friseuse. Sie ist nicht…
   c. Rudi Dessau ist Bauarbeiter. Er ist nicht…
   d. Andreas Freitag ist Kassierer. Er ist nicht…
3. 1. a; 2. d; 3. f; 4. b; 5. c; 6. e
4. a. Ja, ich bin Kellner/Kellnerin.
   b. Ja, ich bin Verkäufer/Verkäuferin.
   c. Ja, ich bin Lehrer/Lehrerin.
   d. Ja, ich bin Professor/Professorin.
   e. Ja, ich bin Kassierer/Kassiererin.
   f. Ja, ich bin Arzt/Ärztin or Krankenpfleger/Krankenpflegerin.
   (If you know other job titles, you may have different answers.)

Pages 43–45

1. *All except German and Spanish. Translations: English, French, Italian, Turkish, Russian, Polish*
2. Deutsch: Deutscher/Deutsche, Österreicher/in, Schweizer/in
   Englisch: Amerikaner/in, Australier/in, Brite/Britin, Kanadier/in
   Französisch: Franzose/Französin, Kanadier/in, Schweizer/in
   Italienisch: Italiener/in, Schweizer/in
   Polnisch: Pole/Polin
   Russisch: Russe/Russin
   Spanisch: Spanier/in
   Türkisch: Türke/Türkin
3. a. Land: Österreich; Muttersprache: Deutsch; Fremdsprachen: etwas Italienisch; Alter: 25; Familienstand: ledig
   b. Staatsangehörigkeit: Türkisch; Muttersprache: Türkisch; Fremdsprachen: Englisch; Alter: 27

c. Land: Deutschland; Staatsangehörigkeit: Schweizerisch; Fremdsprachen: Englisch, Französisch; Familienstand: geschieden

4. *Free answers, but make sure that you have the right details on the right lines:*

Name:	Walsh
Vorname:	Roy
Straße/Nr.:	Crown Road 89
PLZ/Wohnort:	WD6 8LA Watford
Land:	England
Staatsangehörigkeit:	britisch/englisch
Muttersprache:	Englisch
Fremdsprachen:	Deutsch, Schwedisch
Alter:	51
Familienstand:	geschieden

5. *Free answers, of course, but here's our model answer:*

Guten Tag, ich bin/heiße Roy Walsh.

Ich bin Engländer. Ich wohne in Watford, England.

Ich spreche Deutsch und etwas Schwedisch.

Ich bin einundfünfzig Jahre alt und geschieden.

Unit 4

Pages 50–52

1. a. 123; b. 117; c. 217; d. 219

2. 201 zweihunderteins;
221 zweihunderteinundzwanzig;
199 (ein)hundertneunundneunzig;
257 zweihundertsiebenundfünfzig;
375 dreihundertfünfundsiebzig;
999 neunhundertneunundneunzig

3.

1	2	3
80,–	60,–	90,–
110,–	75,–	120,–
ja	ja	*not given*
ja	ja	*not given*
ja	ja	nein

4. Ja, haben Sie ein Doppelzimmer frei?
Drei Nächte.
Ist Frühstück inklusive?
Ich nehme es. (Wir nehmen es.)

5. *Free answers, but here's our model answer:*

Familienname:	Kowalski
Vorname:	Robert
Anschrift	
Straße/Nummer:	1234 Bright Street
PLZ/Wohnort:	10098 New York
Land:	USA
Ausweisnummer:	019670084

Pages 54–56

1. a. die Post, der Zeitungshändler;
b. der Blumenladen; c. das Restaurant;
d. das Café, das Restaurant;
e. der Zeitungshändler, die Buchhandlung;
f. die Post, die Bank, der Geldautomat

2. a. eine; b. ein; c. ein; d. eine; e. ein;
f. ein; g. eine; h. ein

3. 1. a; 2. c; 3. b; 4. d; 5. d; 6. e; 7. a;
8. c

4. a. U-Bahn-Station Uhlandstraße;
b. Café Dreiklang; c. Hotel Spreewald;
d. Taxistand; e. Bäckerei; f. Telefonzelle

5. a. Wie bitte?
b. Wie war das nochmal?
c. Langsamer, bitte!
d. Wie heißt die Straße?
e. Können Sie das buchstabieren?
f. Ich verstehe nicht.

Pages 58–60

1. A. ein
B. ein/zwei.
C. zwei Uhr
D. zwei/zwei
E. zwei/drei
F. Es ist drei Uhr.
G. Es ist zwei Uhr dreißig./Es ist halb drei.
H. drei Uhr /Viertel/vier

2. 6.30; 8.00; 13.30; 15.00; 19.30; 22.00

3. a. Montag; b. Dienstag; c. Mittwoch;
d. Donnerstag; e. Freitag;
f. Samstag/Sonnabend; g. Sonntag

4. 1. Universitäts-Bibliothek; 2. Stadtmuseum;
3. Touristen-Information

5. Wir haben montags bis freitags von neun
(Uhr) bis sechzehn Uhr geöffnet.

Wir haben samstags von neun (Uhr) bis
achtzehn Uhr geöffnet.

Sonntags haben wir geschlossen. (*It would
also be correct to say:* "Sonntag ist
Ruhetag.")

Unit 5

Pages 66–68

1. b, c, a, e, g, h

2. a. Wo kann ich (hier) eine Zeitung kaufen?

b. Wo kann ich (hier) einen Kugelschreiber
kaufen?

c. Wo kann ich (hier) Kopfschmerztabletten
kaufen?

d. Wo kann ich (hier) Obst kaufen?

e. Wo kann ich (hier) Briefmarken kaufen?

f. Wo kann ich (hier) Brot kaufen?

3. a. Obsthändler; b. Bäckerei;
c. Zeitungshändler; d. Apotheke;
e. Schreibwarenladen; f. Post

4. 1. Gehen Sie die zweite Straße rechts und
dann die erste Straße links. Dort ist ein Café.

2. Gehen Sie die dritte Straße links. Dort ist
ein Supermarkt.

*(You may have phrased your answers slightly
differently.)*

5.   ETAGENPLAN

sechste Etage: Dachterrassen-Café

erste Etage: Damenmode und Damenwäsche

fünfte Etage: Elektrogeräte und Computer

dritte Etage: Haushaltswaren und Porzellan

zweite Etage: Herrenmode und Herrenwäsche

Erdgeschoss: Kosmetika und Parfümerie

vierte Etage: Spielwaren und Sportartikel

Pages 70–72

1.

2. *Sabine is child d.*

3. -en (weißen); -e (weiße); -es (weißes)

4. a. Ich suche eine blaue Hose/einen blauen
Rock.

Ich habe Größe *[your size]*.

b. Ich suche eine grüne Bluse/ein grünes
Hemd.

Ich habe Größe *[your size]*.

Pages 73–75

1. a. Im dritten Stock; b. In der vierten Etage;
c. Im Erdgeschoss

2. a. Im fünften Stock./In der fünften Etage./
Im fünften Geschoss.

b. Im zweiten Stock./In der zweiten Etage./
Im zweiten Geschoss.

c. Im Erdgeschoss.

d. Im ersten Stock./In der ersten Etage./
Im ersten Geschoss.

3. Er nimmt den kleinen Teddy, die mittelgroße
Puppe, das rosarote Schwein und die kleinen
Autos.

4. Positive: Ausgezeichnet! Klasse! Prima! Toll!
Wunderschön!

Negative: Hässlich! Igitt! Schrecklich!

Unit 6

Pages 80–82

1. c, a, d, b

2. 1. h; 2. c; 3. f; 4. a; 5. d; 6. c

3. a. Der Zug fährt um 11.46 (elf Uhr
sechsundvierzig).

   b. Man muß in Mannheim umsteigen.

   c. Die Fahrt kostet 137 (einhundertsiebenunddreißig) Euro insgesamt.

   d. Der Zuschlag kostet 20 (zwanzig) Euro.

   e. Der Zug fährt auf Gleis zwei ab.

4. Einmal Hamburg–Altona einfach, bitte.

Zweite Klasse.

(Ich fahre) mit dem ICE.

5. a. Zweimal Berlin hin und zurück, bitte.

   Zweite Klasse.

   (Ich fahre) mit dem ICE.

   Wann fährt der Zug?

   Danke. (Auf) Wiedersehen!

   b. Einmal Frankfurt einfach, bitte.

   Erste Klasse.

   (Ich fahre) mit dem ICE.

   Wann fährt der Zug?

   Danke. (Auf) Wiedersehen!

Page 84

1. 1. (Klasse B: 80,– pro Tag x 3 Tage) 240,–; 2. (Klasse D: 97,– pro Tag x 14 Tage) 1358,–

2. Ich möchte einen mittleren Kombi mieten.

Für sieben Tage.

Bitte schön. Ist das Kilometergeld inbegriffen (inklusive)?

3. 1. *Prohibition* (dürfen Sie nicht);
2. *Prohibition* (darf man nicht);
3. *Obligation* (müssen x 2);
4. *Permission* (darf ich, Sie dürfen) *and obligation* (Sie müssen)

4. a. darf; b. muss; c. darf; d. darf

Pages 87–88

1. a. 3; b. 7; c. 8; d. 7

2. a. Fahren Sie mit der U2 Richtung Spandau.

   b. Fahren Sie mit der U2 Richtung Spandau.

   c. Nehmen Sie die U2 Richtung Spandau bis Potsdamer Platz. Dann nehmen Sie die S1 Richtung Oranienburg.

3. 1. c; 2. b; 3. c; 4. d; 5. d; 6. a

4. a. Fahrschein im Bus entwerten.

   b. Geld einwerfen.

   c. Wechselgeld und Fahrschein nehmen.

   d. Fahrschein wählen.

Extra 1

1. a. (London) BA 456; b. (Moscow) LH 7245;
c. (New York) AA 1230; d. (Paris) AF 1170;
e. (Rome) LH 7256; f. (Sydney) QA 2370

2.

✈ ABFLUG					
Flugnummer	nach/über	Abflug planmäßig	erwartet	Flugsteig	Kommentar
AA 1230	New York	1540	1540	10	Einstieg
BA 456	London H	1550	1550	2	Einstieg
QA 2370	Sydney	1605	1605	7	Abfert.
LH 7245	Moskau	1615	1615	15	Abfert.
AF 1170	Paris	1625	1655	–	verspätet
LH 7256	Rom	1630	1630	12	Abfert.

3. a. Ja, sie wohnt in Berlin. b. Sie kommt aus Hannover. c. Er kommt aus München. d. Er wohnt in Berlin.

4. 1. c; 2. a; 3. b

5. Kiel; Rostock; Schwerin; Hamburg; Bremen; Hannover; Berlin; Dortmund; Köln; Bonn; Erfurt; Leipzig; Dresden; Frankfurt; Saarbrücken; Heidelberg; Nürnberg; Stuttgart; München; Basel; Zürich; Bern; Genf; Innsbruck; Salzburg; Linz; Wien; Graz

Extra 2

1. a. —,89; b. 1,79; c. Orangensaft; d. ,59; e. 2,50; f. das Vollkornbrot

2. a. Flasche; b. einen; c. Kilo; d. Dosen; e. eine; f. ein

3. *Free answers, but you should have something like this:*

Einen Bienenstich, bitte.

Einen Kaffee.

Nein, danke.

Extra 3

1. a. Schwerin; b. Christa, Jörg, Jutta, Manuela, Uwe; c. Jutta; d. *He's her brother*; e. *She's her mother*; f. *She's his grandmother*; g. *She's his daughter*.

2. Dank; Familie; zweiunddreißig; verheiratet; Potsdam; Tochter; sieben; Tierärztin; Heilpraktiker; sprechen; Englisch; Urlaub; USA; Fotos

3. *Photo c. doesn't belong.*

4. *Free answers:*

   Edinburgh, den 19. November

   Liebe Inge,

   vielen Dank für den netten Brief. Ich möchte jetzt etwas von mir und meiner Familie erzählen. Ich bin einundsechzig Jahre alt und mit Jonathan verheiratet. Wir sind beide Rentner. Wir wohnen seit dreißig Jahren hier in Edinburgh, aber ich komme aus Inverness und mein Mann kommt aus Glasgow. Wir haben drei Söhne, Max, Peter und James, und eine Enkeltochter, Katie. Sie ist drei Jahre alt.

   Wir sprechen beide Deutsch und Jonathan spricht auch Französisch und Russisch. Wir machen manchmal Urlaub in Österreich, und möchten in die Schweiz fahren.

   Liebe Grüße,

   Ihre Karen McDonald

Extra 4

1. c

2. a. E; b. C; c.D; d. B; e. A

3. a. Gedächtniskirche; b. Siegessäule; c. Kongresshalle; d. Brandenburger Tor. *The* Fernsehturm *(television tower) is the one which doesn't belong: it's on Alexanderplatz, further to the east.*

Extra 5

1. c.

2. a.

3. *Free answers, but here's our wish list:*

   Ich wünsche mir einen neuen Computer, einen Fotoapparat, zwei gestreifte Hemden und einen Pullover.

4. blaues; rote; orange; grünen; rosa rote; gelben; weiße; grüne

Extra 6

1. b, d

2. Östlich von Magdeburg auf der A2: Ein Unfall ist passiert; Westlich von Magdeburg: Ein Stau bildet sich; Auf der A19 um Güstrow: Nebel; Auf der E45 südlich von Hamburg: Ein Unfall ist passiert: Nördlich von Berlin auf der A24: Verspätungen

3. Bregenzer Str.

Test 1

1. 1. CURRYWURST; 2. STÜCK; 3. KÄNNCHEN; 4. PROBIEREN; 5. BIER; 6. ICH; 7. WURST; 8. SAHNE; 9. HABEN; 10. SEIN; 11. ETWAS

2. a. siebenunddreißig; b. zweiundsechzig; c. neununddreißig; d. fünfundfünfzig; e. dreiundzwanzig

3. a. ist, kommt, spricht, ist, hat, heißt; b. heiße, komme, spreche, bin, habe; c. bin, ist, kommen, haben, heißen

4. 1. Tochter, Söhne; 2. Geschwister, Schwester, Bruder; 3. Mann; 4. Kinder; 5. Mutter, Vater; 6. Großmutter, Großvater; 7. Frau; 8. Enkelkinder

5. a. Sylvia kommt aus England. Sie ist Engländerin. Sie spricht Englisch.

   b. Bob kommt aus den USA. Er ist Amerikaner. Er spricht Englisch.

   c. Jasmin kommt aus der Türkei. Sie ist Türkin. Sie spricht Türkisch.

   d. Hans kommt aus Deutschland. Er ist Deutscher. Er spricht Deutsch.

   e. Isabelle kommt aus Frankreich. Sie ist Französin. Sie spricht Französisch.

f. Marco kommt aus Italien. Er ist Italiener. Er spricht Italienisch.

g. Will kommt aus Australien. Er ist Australier. Er spricht Englisch.

h. Mikhail kommt aus Russland. Er ist Russe. Er spricht Russisch.

i. Delphine kommt aus der Schweiz. Sie ist Schweizerin. Sie spricht Französisch.

j. Erika kommt aus Österreich. Sie ist Österreicherin. Sie spricht Deutsch.

6. a. Dieter Hanschke ist Bauarbeiter. b. Jürgen Schumacher ist Friseur. c. Birgit Harms ist Lehrerin. d. Uwe Balzer ist Krankenpfleger. e. Renate Bachmann ist Kassiererin.

7.
```
A U F E D R S E H E H O Ü H
U U Ü R G U T E N T A G G I
F Ö F G A T Ö R E H L T H T
R G A W U T S T L N L S A T
E D U J I T E C S S O E K C
U D U T M E E A H C H R C H
T W A T E T D N A Ü E V I Ü
M T I S E N G E A U S U A N
I A S E I N M N R C A S O H
C D T C Y S M O S H H B Ü H
H D H F W E T O R R Ö T S T
F T E N A B E D R G Ö R H G
A U F W I E D E R S E H E N
U F W I E D E H Ü S S N E N
```

Test 2

1. *Across:* 1. UMSTEIGEN; 3. FAHRSCHEIN; 4. ZURÜCK; 5. VERSICHERUNG; 6. RICHTUNG; 7. ABFAHRT; 9. GLEIS; 10. EINMAL

   Down: 2. EINBAHNSTRASSE; 3. FAHRE; 4. ZUSCHLAG; 7. ALLE; 8. GEHEN

2. a. Ich suche einen roten Rock.

   b. Ich suche eine grüne Hose.

   c. Ich suche eine schwarze Jacke.

   d. Ich suche ein weißes Hemd.

   e. Ich suche einen blauen Pullover.

3. Elektrogeräte: Computer; Spielwaren: Puppe, Teddy; Schreibwaren: Kugelschreiber; Damenmode: Rock, Bluse; Herrenmode: Herrenhose, Schlips; Kosmetika: Parfüm; Lebensmittel: Brot, Fleisch

4. Guten Tag. Kann ich etwas für Sie tun?

   Ja. Wir möchten ein Doppelzimmer mit Dusche.

   Wie lange möchten Sie bleiben?

   Wir möchten drei Nächte bleiben.

   Ja, wir haben ein Doppelzimmer frei. Das kostet einhundertzehn Euro pro Nacht.

   Ist Frühstück inbegriffen?

   Ja, Frühstück ist inbegriffen.

   Wir nehmen es.

   Füllen Sie bitte das Formular aus. OR: Füllen Sie das Formular aus, bitte.

5. a. Es ist Viertel nach acht.

   b. Die Bibliothek öffnet von neun Uhr dreißig bis neunzehn Uhr dreißig.

   c. Der Zug nach Freiburg fährt um siebzehn Uhr zehn.

   d. Ich komme (Wir kommen) um halb sechs in München an.

   e. Die Nachrichten kommen um Viertel vor sechs.

6. a. Steigen Sie in Mannheim um.

   b. Fahren Sie geradeaus, biegen Sie dann links ein.

   c. Werfen Sie das Geld ein.

   d. Entwerten Sie den Fahrschein im Bus.

   e. Fahren Sie um elf Uhr ab.

7. Rennfahrer, Ruhetag, Geldautomat, Taxistand, Damenmode, Erdgeschoss, Schreibwarenladen, Neuseeland

Notes